Green Finance and Investment

Mobilising Finance for Climate Action in Georgia

This work is published under the responsibility of the Secretary-General of the OECD. The opinions expressed and arguments employed herein do not necessarily reflect the official views of OECD member countries.

This document, as well as any data and any map included herein, are without prejudice to the status of or sovereignty over any territory, to the delimitation of international frontiers and boundaries and to the name of any territory, city or area.

Please cite this publication as:
OECD (2018), *Mobilising Finance for Climate Action in Georgia*, Green Finance and Investment, OECD Publishing, Paris.
http://dx.doi.org/10.1787/9789264289727-en

ISBN 978-92-64-28970-3 (print)
ISBN 978-92-64-28972-7 (PDF)

Series: Green Finance and Investment
ISSN 2409-0336 (print)
ISSN 2409-0344 (online)

The statistical data for Israel are supplied by and under the responsibility of the relevant Israeli authorities. The use of such data by the OECD is without prejudice to the status of the Golan Heights, East Jerusalem and Israeli settlements in the West Bank under the terms of international law.

Corrigenda to OECD publications may be found on line at: *www.oecd.org/about/publishing/corrigenda.htm*.
© OECD 2018

You can copy, download or print OECD content for your own use, and you can include excerpts from OECD publications, databases and multimedia products in your own documents, presentations, blogs, websites and teaching materials, provided that suitable acknowledgment of the source and copyright owner(s) is given. All requests for public or commercial use and translation rights should be submitted to *rights@oecd.org*. Requests for permission to photocopy portions of this material for public or commercial use shall be addressed directly to the Copyright Clearance Center (CCC) at *info@copyright.com* or the Centre francais d'exploitation du droit de copie (CFC) at *contact@cfcopies.com*.

Foreword

The nationally determined contribution (NDC) of Georgia, communicated to the United Nations Framework Convention on Climate Change (UNFCCC), stresses that substantially limiting Georgia's greenhouse gas (GHG) emissions to meet its climate goals requires greater investments in low-carbon technologies throughout the country. More broadly, Georgia's Socio-Economic Development Strategy – "Georgia 2020" – provides a clear vision for development. The strategy highlights three key principles: fast and efficient economic growth; inclusive economic growth, envisaging the universal involvement of the population in the development process; and rational use of natural resources, ensuring environmental safety and sustainability and avoiding natural disasters. All of them inevitably require further policy reforms to mobilise various sources of finance for economic growth that is green, stable and inclusive.

This report focuses primarily on challenges and opportunities regarding further mobilisation of finance for climate action in Georgia. It focuses particularly on climate change mitigation, from various sources, especially private-sector finance that is mobilised by public interventions. Climate-related issues are closely linked to other environmental and energy-related issues, such as air quality, energy security and access, and waste management, among others. Thus, the analysis may also provide insight into finance for other issues around the country's green growth agenda. Such issues may include energy productivity; air pollution prevention; better waste management; conservation of natural resources and ecosystems; and technologies and innovations that help tackle the issues above.

This report is structured as follows. Chapter 1 provides a summary of background information and highlights key findings and a potential way-forward based on analysis in the subsequent chapters. Chapter 2 takes stock of various estimates of financial needs for pursuing Georgia's climate action, based on publicly available information. Chapter 3 outlines key climate policies and targets in Georgia, which are critical to create demand for investment in climate action. Chapter 4 maps and discusses the existing and potential sources of finance for climate action in Georgia to meet the demand. Chapter 5 reviews several policy domains; these may not have been designed to address climate change risks, but can significantly help make it easier to mobilise finance for climate action in the country.

This report was prepared as part of the project "International Climate Finance for Eastern Europe, the Caucasus, Central Asia", supported by the German Federal Ministry for the Environment, Nature Conservation, Building and Nuclear Safety and implemented by the GREEN Action Task Force hosted by the Organisation for Economic Co-operation and Development (OECD).

Analytical methodologies are based on approaches in various OECD work, including OECD (2017), *Investing in Climate, Investing in Growth*; OECD-IEA-ITF-NEA (2015), *Aligning Policies for a Low-carbon Economy*; and OECD (2015), *Policy Guidance for Investment in Clean Energy Infrastructure*, as well as various ongoing work under the

OECD Centre on Green Finance and Investment (www.oecd.org/cgfi/). The information sources are policy-related documents and database that are publicly available or those provided by the government of Georgia. The OECD also consulted with a range of Georgian stakeholders in both private and public sectors. It also sought input from development co-operation partners, including multilateral and bilateral providers of finance and support. Stakeholder consultations involved semi-structured bilateral and online interviews between February and April in 2017, as well as email exchanges. Input was also provided at a "Policy Dialogue on Green Economy in Georgia: Workshop on Green Finance Mobilisation" co-organised by the Ministry of Environment and Natural Resources Protection and the OECD in Tbilisi on 22 and 23 June 2017.

Acknowledgements

This report, an output of the OECD Environment Directorate, was written by Takayoshi Kato under the guidance of Kumi Kitamori and Krzysztof Michalak. The OECD-hosted GREEN Action Task Force (www.oecd.org/env/outreach/eap-tf.htm) implemented this project in close collaboration with the Ministry of Environment and Natural Resources Protection, Ministry of Economy and Sustainable Development, and Ministry of Energy of Georgia.

The author is grateful to Ekaterine Grigalava, Deputy Minister of Natural Environment and Natural Resources Protection, and her team: Gizo Chelidze, Grigol Lazrievi, Tamar Aladashvili, Maia Tskhvaradze and Kakhaber Mdivani for their co-operation with the OECD in conducting this project and organising the in-country workshop on green finance mobilisation held on 22-23 June 2017 in Tbilisi.

Development of this report benefited from the substantive and administrative support of Maia Tskhvaradze (Ministry of Environment and Natural Resources Protection). The author also gratefully received substantive input from other Georgian ministries and public-sector institutions. These included the Ministry of Economy and Sustainable Development (Irma Kavtaradze, Davit Advadze, Giorgi Chichinadze and Nino Lazashvili), Ministry of Education and Science (Teimuraz Murgulia), Ministry of Energy (Margalita Arabidze, Natalia Jamburia and Giorgi Sirbiladze), Ministry of Finance (Natia Gulua), National Bank of Georgia (Giorgi Laliashvili and Zviad Zedginidze), Tbilisi City Hall (Nina Khatiskatsi and Elene Khundadze), Georgian Energy Development Fund (Giorgi Chachibaia and Nugzar Khaindrava), LEPL Enterprise Georgia (Kristine Meparishvili and Aleksandre Papiashvili), Municipal Development Fund (Giga Gvelesiani and Davit Tabidze) and Partnership Fund (Nino Cholokashvili).

The author is also thankful to the Bank of Georgia (Tamar Khizanishuvili), Georgian Co-Investment Fund (Irakli Menabde), Georgian Industrial Group (Levan Vepkhvadze), MFO Crystal (Archil Bakuradze, Kakha Gabeskiria and Maya Kobalia), PMO Business Consulting (Levan Gogoladze), ProCredit Bank Georgia (Ioseb Rostomashvili), Remissia (Marina Shvangiradze) and Winrock International Georgia (Giorgi Giorgobiani and Inga Pkhaladze) for their invaluable input and insight from the perspective of the private sector and civil society organisations.

This report also greatly benefited from valuable insights provided by Georgia's development co-operation partners, including: the Asian Development Bank (Yesim Elhan-Kayalar and George Luarsabishvili), European Bank for Reconstruction and Development (Thea Melikadze), European Investment Bank (Cyrille Arnould, Mónica Arévalo Calsina, Maciej Czura, Sébastien Husson de Sampigny and Grigorios Krallis), GIZ (Felix Fallasch, Gvantsa Gverdtsiteli, Mikheil Khuchua, Martina Kolb, and Irakli Samkharadze), Green Climate Fund (Leo Park), Greenhawk Cleantech Advisory (Yoav N. Brandt), IFC (Martin Dasek, Thea Gigiberia, Sophie Lalieva and Tamar Barbakadze), International Association of Public Transport (Hilia Boris), KfW (Nino Shanidze), United Nations Industrial Development Organization (Malkhaz Adeishvili, Tatiana Chernyavskaya, Ana Chorgolashvili, and Marko van Waveren Hogervorst) and World Bank (Joseph Melitauri).

The author gratefully acknowledges written comments on this report from OECD colleagues: Geraldine Ang, Rodney Boyd, Jane Ellis Raphaël Jachnik, Kumi Kitamori, Alexandre Martoussevitch, Lauren McNicoll, Krzysztof Michalak, Dirk Röttgers, David Šimek and Robert Youngman, as well as from colleagues at the International Transport Forum: Aimée Aguilar Jaber and Elene Shatberashvili.

The author also thanks Lupita Johanson and Janine Treves (OECD), who provided advice on communication aspects and helped process the publication; Irina Belkahia and Deborah Holmes-Michel (OECD) who provided administrative support; and Mark Foss who edited the report.

Table of contents

Acronyms and abbreviations 9

Executive summary 13

Chapter 1. **Mobilising finance for climate action in Georgia: Assessment and recommendations** . . 15
    Investment needs for climate action vs. available and potential sources of finance 17
    Ensure coherence between strategic policy documents to mobilise finance for climate action 20
    Create demand for climate-related activities 21
    Improve the capital market and other enabling conditions to meet investment demand 23
    Notes 25
    References 25

Chapter 2. **Investment needs for achieving Georgia's climate targets** 31
    Stocktaking of investment needs for climate action in Georgia 32
    Capital sources to meet the needs: An example from NEEAP 34
    Note 35
    References 35

Chapter 3. **Creating investment needs: Overview of climate policies in Georgia** 37
    Outline of Georgia's nationally determined contribution 38
    Strategic policy documents on climate action and broader development agenda 39
    Need for coherence among policy documents and strong stakeholder engagement 43
    Enhancing environmental regulations to drive investment demand for climate action 45
    Need for energy subsidies reform 48
    Greening public procurement 49
    The level playing field between different renewable energy options 51
    Note 51
    References 51

Chapter 4. **Channels of finance for climate action in Georgia** 55
    Stocktaking of financial channels for climate-related investment 56
    Exploring new financial channels for green finance 67
    References 70

Chapter 5. **Aligning broader enabling conditions for investments with Georgia's climate action** . 75
    Financial market policies 76
    Competition policies 82
    Addressing information gap and enhancing capacity 85
    Notes 86
    References 87

Figures

Figure 1.1	Stocktaking of long-term investment needs (USD million)	18
Figure 1.2	Factors that influence mobilisation of private finance for climate action in Georgia	20
Figure 2.1	Stocktaking of long-term investment needs (USD million)	33
Figure 2.2	Expected financial sources for energy-efficiency measures in NEEAP for 2017-30	35
Figure 3.1	GHG emissions trend and NDC targets	38
Figure 3.2	Expected changes to regulations that would drive demand for resource-efficient and cleaner production	46
Figure 3.3	Trends in energy intensity in Georgia	46
Figure 3.4	Total primary energy supply by fuel (2000-14)	49
Figure 4.1	Investment in fixed capital stock in Georgia (2001-15)	56
Figure 4.2	Volume and growth rate of commercial bank loans in Georgia	60
Figure 4.3	Annual climate-related development finance committed to Georgia in 2013-15	64
Figure 5.1	Interests rates in Georgia	76

Tables

Table 1.1	Green growth indicators in Georgia	17
Table 2.1	Examples of renewable energy projects in Georgia, excluding hydropower	34
Table 3.1	Overview of Georgia's nationally determined contribution	39
Table 3.2	Examples of laws and strategic policy documents relating to climate change action in Georgia	40
Table 3.3	Sector coverage and objectives of national-level strategic documents on green growth and climate action in Georgia	43
Table 3.4	Summary of national-level mitigation policies in Georgia and benchmark countries	47
Table 3.5	Examples of cross-boundary green public procurement initiatives	50
Table 4.1	Examples of financial channels already or potentially available for financing climate action in Georgia	57
Table 4.2	Examples of private-sector investors in renewable energy in Georgia (excluding commercial banks)	63
Table 4.3	Examples of credit line programmes by development financial institutions related to energy efficiency and renewable energy	66
Table 5.1	Examples of issued bonds and their performance	78
Table 5.2	Key factors for developing Georgia's capital market and its status	79
Table 5.3	Examples of risk mitigation instruments	80
Table 5.4	The structure of Georgia's electricity market	83

Boxes

Box 3.1	Financing climate action at the municipal level	42
Box 4.1	Greening the loan operation and management system of Procredit Bank Georgia	61
Box 4.2	JSC m2 Real Estate's investment in electric vehicle chargers	63
Box 4.3	Different types of green bonds	68
Box 4.4	Microfinance Organization Crystal's Green Funding Action Plan	69
Box 5.1	The Energy Community	84

Acronyms and abbreviations

ADB	Asian Development Bank
CCEF	Caucasus Clean Energy Fund
CPLC	Carbon Pricing Leadership Coalition
CRS	Creditors Reporting System
DCFTA	Deep and Comprehensive Free Trade Area
DEG	German Investment and Development Company
EBRD	European Bank for Reconstruction and Development
EC-LEDS	Enhancing Capacity for Low Emission Development Strategies Program
EIB	European Investment Bank
EMS	Environmental management system
ESCO	Electricity System Commercial Operator
ESG	Environment, Social and Governance
ESMS	Environmental and Social Management System
EU	European Union
EUR	Euros
FDI	Foreign direct investment
FMO	Dutch Development Bank
GCF	Green Climate Fund
GCPF	Global Climate Partnership Fund
GEDF	Georgian Energy Development Fund
GEEREF	Global Energy Efficiency and Renewable Energy Fund
GEL	Georgian Laris
GHG	Greenhouse gas
GIG	Georgian Industrial Group
GNERC	Georgian National Energy and Water Supply Regulatory Commission
GoG	Government of Georgia
GOGC	Georgian Oil and Gas Corporation
GSE	Georgian State Electrosystem

HPP	Hydropower plant
IDB	Inter-American Development Bank
IEA	International Energy Agency
IFC	International Finance Corporation
ILO	International Labour Organization
IMF	International Monetary Fund
IPCC	Intergovernmental Panel on Climate Change
ITF	International Transport Forum
JSC	Joint Stock Company
KTCF	Korea Technical Assistance and Cooperation Fund
LEDS	Low Emission Development Strategy
LULUCF	Land use, land-use change and forestry
MDBs	Multilateral development banks
MFI	Microfinance institution
MFO	Microfinance organisation
MIGA	Multilateral Investment Guarantee Agency
MoENRP	Ministry of Environment and Natural Resources Protection
MoESD	Ministry of Economy and Sustainable Development of Georgia
MPSF	Municipal Project Support Facility
$MtCO_2$	1 000 000 tonnes of CO_2
NAMAs	Nationally Appropriate Mitigation Actions
NAP	National adaptation plan
NBG	National Bank of Georgia
NDC	Nationally determined contribution
NEA	Nuclear Energy Agency
NEEAP	National Energy Efficiency Action Plan
NIF	Neighbourhood Investment Facility
OeEB	Austrian Development Bank
PPA	Power purchase agreement
PPP	Purchasing power parity
SACE	Servizi Assicurativi del Commercio Estero (the Italian Export Credit Agency)
SEAPs	Sustainable Energy Action Plans
SMEs	Small and medium-sized enterprises
SPV	Special purpose vehicles

TA	Technical Assistance
toe	tonne of oil equivalent
TPES	Total primary energy supply
TPP	Thermal power plant
UNDP	United Nations Development Programme
UNECE	United Nations Economic Commission for Europe
UNFCCC	United Nations Framework Convention on Climate Change
UNIDO	United Nations Industrial Development Organization
USAID	United States Agency for International Development
USD	United States dollars
VAT	Value-added tax
WPP	Wind power plant

Executive summary

Georgia has undertaken a wide range of economic reforms, significantly improving economic and social indicators. However, its environmental performance has lagged. In response, the government of Georgia and Georgian municipalities, often in collaboration with development co-operation partners, have been actively developing policy for climate action and green growth. Policy documents include the nationally determined contribution (NDC), Low Emission Development Strategy (LEDS), National Energy Efficiency Action Plan (NEEAP) and Nationally Appropriate Mitigation Actions (NAMAs). Eleven Georgian municipalities have submitted their own Sustainable Energy Action Plans (SEAPs) under the "Covenant of Mayors" initiative. The government of Georgia has also started developing a Green Economy Strategy, a National Renewable Energy Action Plan and a Climate Action Plan as an implementation strategy for the NDC.

These strategic policy documents make it clear that Georgia needs to further scale up finance from various sources to implement climate action in the country. It is also widely recognised in Georgia that finance for climate action should not only benefit the environment, but also enhance business opportunities, technology transfer and job creation. This, in turn, will contribute to stable and inclusive economic growth. While it is challenging to have a complete picture, the estimated investment needs in some areas are already detailed. These include energy-efficiency measures calculated under NEEAP and LEDS, as well as hydropower projects (about USD 2.4 billion over the same period). Investment needs for other sectors and topics (e.g. non-hydropower renewable energy and adaptation) remain less detailed or unavailable.

The availability of low-cost, long-term capital, especially from the private sector, in Georgia is limited. This severely hampers investments in climate- and environment-related projects and other types of fixed assets. The potential for investment is also exacerbated by high collateral requirements, information gaps in available technologies and financial products, and limited capacities in both providers and recipients of finance in Georgia, among other factors. Finance for climate action from commercial banks, institutional investors and businesses does exist. However, it is largely concentrated on hydropower; mobilisation of finance for energy efficiency from these sources remains limited. A national-level, central data depository could partly help solve the issues around information gaps. Such a depository could collect, collate and maintain information on, for example, loan-level data, performance track records of investment projects and technologies, and hydro-meteorological data.

Despite progress in policy development, the government of Georgia, together with the National Bank of Georgia (the country's central bank) and other public and private financial institutions, needs further reforms. Revamped policies should enable finance to flow to achieve Georgia's targets on climate change and green growth. Such effort is needed to drive demand for investment in climate action within the country. It also needs to enhance the financial system, other sectoral policies and enabling conditions, which are conducive to meeting the demand for such finance.

Creating demand for investment in climate action relies on a strong and stable policy signal, reasonably stringent environmental regulations and their enforcement, and effective communication to, and engagement with, stakeholders. Georgian enterprises, from small- to large-sized ones, consider stricter environmental policies to be the most important lever for an investment decision e.g. resource efficiency and cleaner production measures. Georgia's State Procurement Agency can also consider "greening" its public procurement system to promote investment in climate action and to trigger industrial and business model innovation.

Ensuring coherence among existing and upcoming climate- and green growth-related strategic policy documents will be crucial to create the demand for finance. Such policy coherence can help build confidence among Georgian stakeholders, in both public and private sectors, to direct their financial resources to climate action. Better coherence will also help the government of Georgia avoid inefficiency and unexpected obstacles. Further, it will reduce confusion among relevant stakeholders around implementation of strategic measures. Financing climate action is needed at both national and municipal levels. Municipalities (including large cities such as Tbilisi and Batumi) face severe financial constraints to improve environmental quality and efficiency of their public infrastructure such as transport and public buildings.

Further rationalising the energy prices in Georgia will greatly help mobilise finance for energy-efficiency measures and smaller-scale renewable projects (e.g. decentralised solar power). Although the Georgian government has indeed taken steps to increase tax rates on certain fossil fuels (e.g. amendments to the Tax Code in 2017), energy prices remain too low to attract finance for the measures mentioned above. Nonetheless, issues around energy affordability for end-users often make energy subsidy reforms political sensitive as in many other countries.

On the supply side of finance, a broader range of capital channels than collateral lending would help lower financial cost and complement commercial bank loans, including for climate action in Georgia, over time. The government of Georgia and the central bank are making progress in reforming the country's financial market (e.g. securities market, money market and payment system). This could help develop a comprehensive financial sector conducive to green finance mobilisation. Establishing a green bank/fund, or strengthening an existing sovereign equity fund, could help investors mitigate financial risks and costs associated with climate-related projects.

Interest in green bonds is increasing in Georgia, although none has been issued as of August 2017. Challenges still exist, such as scalability of projects and the nascent bond market in Georgia. The government, in collaboration with, for instance, the central bank and the Georgian Stock Exchange, can develop its green bond standard or adopt an existing one(s) developed by other institutions or countries.

Microfinance institutions, institutional investors and non-financial sector corporations could play a greater part in financial flows to climate action in Georgia. Some microfinance institutions and commercial banks are making progress in designing and providing loan products for climate action.

The government of Georgia should fully seize opportunities that stem from the Energy Community Treaty to drive further development of the competitive electricity market. Such a market, if designed properly, can create further space for investments in renewable energy and energy efficiency. In parallel, state-owned enterprises in the energy sector, such as the Electricity System Commercial Operator, the Georgian State Electrosystem, and the Energotrans LLC could also promote the government's green growth agenda.

Chapter 1

Mobilising finance for climate action in Georgia: Assessment and recommendations

This chapter describes challenges and opportunities regarding further mobilising finance for climate action in Georgia, based on analysis in subsequent chapters. It examines investment needs for climate action vs. potential and available sources of finance, recognising that climate action should benefit both the environment and the economy. It highlights the importance of coherence among several strategic policy documents on climate change and green growth. It also assesses creating demand for financing climate action through enhanced policies and regulations. Finally, it examines development of the financial market and other enabling conditions conducive to further mobilisation of finance for climate action in the country.

Over the past 15 years, Georgia has undertaken a range of drastic reforms, including a restructuring of the public sector, deregulation for businesses, a fight against corruption and streamlining of tax- and trade-related rules and procedures. The improved legal framework and capacity of the public sector has generated several positive results over the past decade. These include strong gross domestic product (GDP) growth, increased foreign direct investment (FDI) inflows and macroeconomic stability. The Georgian economy has proven its strength and resilience even during various external economic and political shocks in the late 2000s. While the country suffers from slow economic growth in recent years, its 2.7% GDP growth in 2016 was higher than the average of Eastern Europe, the Caucasus and Central Asia (EECCA), as well as Turkey and the Russian Federation (1.0%) (World Bank, 2017a). In addition, the poverty rate, while still significant, fell from 46.7% to 31.5% over 2010-15,[1] driven by higher labour income and redistributive fiscal policy (World Bank, 2017b).

At the same time, although Georgia has made efforts to reform its environmental policies in recent years, the pursuit of simpler regulations has partly kept policies on energy use and environmental quality relatively lenient. Such policies, for example, target environmental safeguards and regulation, as well as market-based mechanisms such as pollution charges (OECD, 2016a; UNECE, 2016). This leniency has been exacerbated by the limited domestic capacity and capability of the public sector, including the government bodies in charge of environmental regulations and policy making. Examples of challenges are diverse. The level of air pollution remains high, including from the urban transport systems and automobiles. The energy intensity of the economy is also high, including at buildings and industrial facilities. Soil erosion is a critical threat to Georgia's soils. Municipal wastewater pollutes surface water. The sea level rise of the Black Sea is likely to damage the coastal infrastructure (GoG, 2015a; UNECE, 2016; IEA, 2017). Table 1.1. outlines some key indicators relating to Georgia's green growth.

Having been recognised as a major threat to Georgia's long-term socio-economic development, environmental issues, including climate change, have gained momentum on the country's political agenda. The government has been determined to pursue economic growth that is green, stable and inclusive (GoG, 2014). To that end, the country is increasingly developing policy on climate change and green growth. Indeed, Georgia's Socio-Economic Development Strategy "Georgia 2020" adopted in 2014 highlights three key principles of economic development. These principles are fast and efficient economic growth; inclusive economic growth, envisaging the universal involvement of the population in the development process; and rational use of natural resources, ensuring environmental safety and sustainability and avoiding natural disasters (GoG, 2014).

Regarding its climate action, Georgia has communicated internationally its climate targets through its nationally determined contribution (NDC). It has also developed key strategic documents such as the Low Emission Development Strategy (LEDS), National Energy Efficiency Action Plan (NEEAP) and Nationally Appropriate Mitigation Actions (NAMAs), among others.[2] Through the NDC, Georgia commits 15% of greenhouse gas (GHG) reductions below business as usual (BAU) by 2030. Further, it has committed 25% of reductions below BAU, contingent on international support with finance and technology. As well, 11 Georgian self-governing cities and municipalities have submitted their own Sustainable Energy Action Plans (SEAPs) under the European Union's "Covenant of Mayors" initiative, aiming to reduce their GHG emissions voluntarily (Covenant of Mayors, 2017). As of 2017, 18 self-governing cities and municipalities are signatories to this initiative. Georgia also plans more policy documents such as a Green Economy Strategy, led by the Ministry of Economy and Sustainable Development. The Ministry of Energy will also lead a National Renewable Energy Action Plan. And the Ministry of Environment and Natural

Resources Protection will lead a Climate Action Plan as the NDC implementation strategy (Chapters 3.1 and 3.2)

Finance is a crucial enabler for implementing these policy documents above. This report focuses on challenges and opportunities regarding further mobilisation of finance for climate action in the country, particularly for climate change mitigation. It looks at various sources of finance for climate action, especially private-sector finance that is mobilised by public interventions. The analysis also provides insight into how finance can address other issues around the country's green growth agenda. Such issues include energy productivity; air pollution prevention; water supply and sanitation; better waste management; conservation of natural resources; and technologies and innovations that help tackle the issues above. Climate risks are closely linked to other environmental and energy-related issues mentioned above, hence tackling climate change issues typically helps address these types of problems as well.

Table 1.1. **Green growth indicators in Georgia**

	2000	Latest year available
GDP growth (annual percentage)	1.8	2.8 (2015)
GDP per capita (PPP, constant 2011 international $)	1 438.7	4 010.3 (2015)
Unemployment (percentage of total labour force) (ILO estimate)	10.8	13.4 (2014)
Gini Index (World Bank)	40.5	40.1 (2014)
CO_2 productivity (US dollars per kilogram of energy-related CO_2 emissions, 2010)	3.1	4.1 (2014)
Energy productivity (GDP per unit of US Dollar, 2010)	4 931.0	7 277.7 (2014)
Renewable energy (percentage of TPES)	40.3	27.3 (2014)
Forest area (percentage of land area)	39.7	40.6 (2015)
Agriculture land (percentage of land area)	43.2	36.8 (2014)
Mean population exposure to PM2.5	16.9	15.9 (2013)
Development of environment-related technologies (percentage of all technologies)	9.6	7.9 (2012)

Source: Based on OECD (2017c) and World Bank (2017d).

Investment needs for climate action vs. available and potential sources of finance

Georgia has developed several strategic policy documents for climate action recently, including the NDC, LEDS and NEEAP. They make it clear that Georgia will need to further scale up finance for climate action from various sources. Sectors and activities that require finance for their climate action are diverse. Chapter 2 takes stock of publicly available information on various estimated financial needs for energy use (e.g. buildings and industry), energy supply (generation and distribution) and transport. It also takes stock of investment needs for land use, land-use change and forestry (LULUCF), non-energy related GHG emissions (e.g. agriculture, industrial process and waste) and climate change adaptation, which are also summarised in Figure 1.1.

It is widely recognised in Georgia that finance for climate action should not only benefit the environment, but also enhance business opportunities, technology transfer and job creation. This, in turn, will contribute to stable and inclusive economic growth. Some Georgian companies have already started to see "green" investments as an opportunity. They have begun diversifying their business portfolios and strengthening their competitive advantages in the emerging new business contexts such as the Georgia-EU Deep and Comprehensive Free Trade Area (DCFTA) and the Association Agreement with the

European Union (EU). For instance, JSC Partnership Fund, a sovereign equity fund, has invested in the facility that produces energy-efficient construction material (building blocks) in Ytong Caucasus for the Georgian market (Partnership Fund, 2016). Georgia's obligation as part of the Association Agreement to ensure energy-efficient construction has driven this investment decision. Further, the Association Agreement also necessitates further investment in development and upgrading of a range of infrastructure in, for instance, water supply and sanitation, waste water management and electricity sectors. Many projects in these sectors can be closely linked to the country's climate and green growth agendas as well. (Chapter 4.1.)

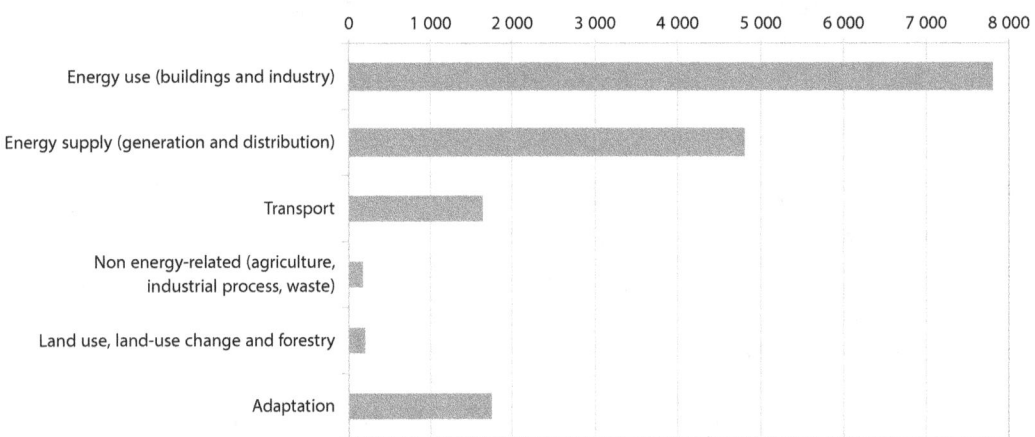

Figure 1.1. **Stocktaking of long-term investment needs (USD million)**

Notes: 1. Further disaggregated estimates are available in Figure 2.1 in Chapter 2.1.
2. Cost estimate methodologies may differ among the information sources. Therefore, this figure does not aggregate numbers across sectors.

Source: Author's calculation, based on GoG (2015a, 2015b); GEDF (2017); NEEAP Expert Team (2017); and Winrock and Remmisia (2017).

Estimates of investment needs in some areas are already detailed. For instance, gross investment needs for energy efficiency under NEEAP would be approximately USD 8.3 billion from 2017-30. Some USD 10.6 billion is needed for energy efficiency, non-energy related GHG emissions and LULUCF, among others, for LEDS. Meanwhile, the third National Communication for hydropower projects requires about USD 2.4 billion over the same period (GoG, 2016; NEEAP Expert Team, 2017; Winrock and Remmisia, 2017). The cost estimates for other sectors are less granular or more uncertain (e.g. for "non-hydro" renewable energy and adaptation projects). The NDC shows that adaptation finance will require about USD 1.5-2.0 billion of finance from 2021 to 2030. However, it provides no explanation or reference on how these figures are calculated. Georgia's NDC includes mitigation targets that are contingent on international support. However, it does not show the amount the country will need from international sources (see Chapter 2 for details).

Estimating an accurate national-level figure of financial needs for climate action towards 2030 remains challenging for Georgia and many other countries (OECD, 2017a). Better estimates of investment needs can help the government of Georgia prioritise specific projects in light of the country's targets on climate change and green growth. This is especially true for priority sectors such as energy efficiency, renewable energy, transport and adaptation. Better estimates of needs might also send a stronger signal to potential

investors in these priority projects. Enhancing estimates of financial needs can include the following steps:
- defining what "finance for climate action, or green growth" encompasses
- defining total financial needs for priority programmes and projects as shown above
- identifying financial flows from domestic or international sources or both, depending on the scope of the work (thus tracking the total amount may not be necessary).

Whether labelled as climate-related finance or not, various sources have already provided finance to different areas. This includes, for instance, renewable energy and energy efficiency, as well as climate change adaptation. However, the investment is still insufficient for the amount needed (GoG, 2016, 2015a; NEEAP Expert Team, 2017). Further, financing is lacking particularly for renewable energy other than hydropower, energy efficiency in the public- and private-sector buildings, clean transport systems, and resource efficiency and cleaner production, especially at small and medium-sized enterprises (SMEs) (Chorgolashvili, 2017; Copenhagen Centre on Energy Efficiency, 2017; Singh, et al., 2016; Ministry of Energy, 2017). See also Chapter 4.1.

Limited availability of low-cost, long-term capital in Georgia, especially from the private sector, severely hampers investments in climate-related projects and other types of fixed assets. Some low-interest rate loan products from commercial banks exist, but with the minimum requested amount of GEL 100 000 (about USD 38 600). Typically SMEs need EUR 9 000 to 40 000 for green projects, which does not match with the minimum amount mentioned above (Chorgolashvili, 2017). The high collateral requirement from banks – about 220% of the value of the loan – also makes it difficult for Georgian companies, especially SMEs, to take loans (EU4Business, 2017). A study shows that commercial banks normally do not reach the threshold of uncollateralised loan stipulated by law (25% of total portfolio). This implies that commercial banks perceive a greater level of risk than those required by the regulations (EIB, 2016). A high degree of "dollarisation" of assets in Georgia may also have various implications for mobilising finance for climate action. These implications would be on top of various negative effects on the country's fiscal sustainability and the effectiveness of the monetary policies in general.

The national and municipal governments, state-owned enterprises and development financial institutions are, and likely to remain, the major financial source for climate action. NEEAP, for instance, assumes that more than 40% of finance for energy efficiency will come from domestic public sources including state-owned entities. However, those public finance sources are scarce and should be used wisely so that they can mobilise further private-sector investment and avoid any crowding-out. (Chapter 2).

Finance for climate action from commercial banks, institutional investors and businesses does exist, but is largely concentrated on hydropower. Mobilisation of finance for energy efficiency, "non-hydro" renewable energy and adaptation from these sources remains limited (Chapter 4.1.). Hydropower projects in Georgia have already attracted private-sector investors and lenders both within and outside of the country. This was made possible by revenue guarantees through the power purchase agreements (PPAs) and other preferential policies for renewable energies backed by the government. PPAs have been an essential policy lever for attracting finance in hydropower projects. But they have also led to a high degree of financial liabilities borne by the Georgian government (IMF, 2017). The government is revising the rules on renewable energy development so that it will not issue PPAs in the future but will discuss terms for each project separately and agree on the individual tariff level.

Ensure coherence between strategic policy documents to mobilise finance for climate action

Despite its progress, the government of Georgia, together with the National Bank of Georgia and other public and private financial institutions, needs further policy reforms. These reforms should drive the demand for investment in climate action within the country. They should also build the financial system, other sectoral policies and enabling conditions, which are conducive to meeting the demand for such finance. Figure 1.2 illustrates the interaction between different factors that influence mobilisation of finance for climate action. These factors include direct investment, financial incentives, capacity and knowledge enhancement, particularly investment by private-sector sources. The contents of LEDS and NEEAP also imply the importance of both measures to create demand for climate-related projects, and funding mechanisms to meet the demand.

Figure 1.2. **Factors that influence mobilisation of private finance for climate action in Georgia**

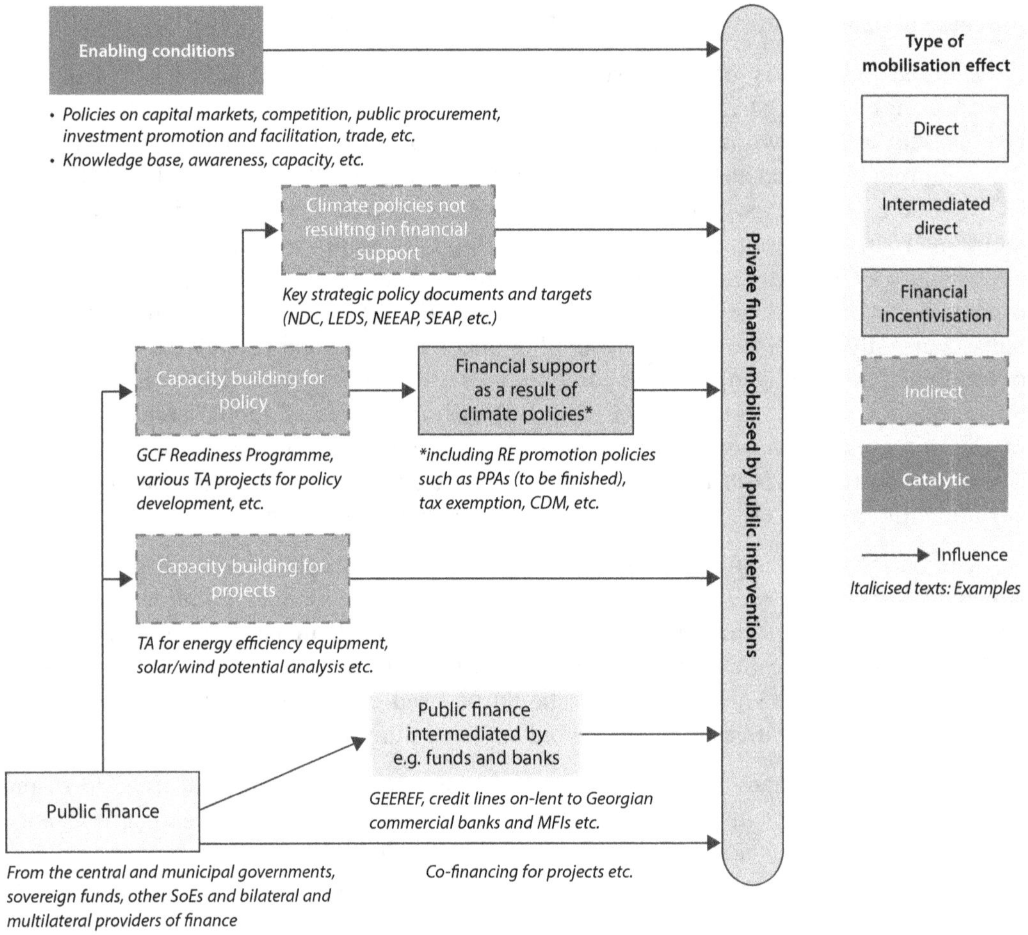

Acronyms: **CDM**: Clean Development Mechanism, **GCF**: the Green Climate Fund, **GEEREF**: Global Energy Efficiency and Renewable Energy Fund, **LEDS**: Low Emission Development Strategy, **MFI**: Microfinance institutions, **NDC**: nationally determined contribution, **NEEAP**: National Energy Efficiency Action Plan, **PPAs**: Power Purchase Agreements, **SEAP**: Sustainable Energy Action Plan, **SoEs**: State-owned Enterprises, **TA**: Technical Assistance.

Source: Author, based on McNicoll & Jachnik (2017).

LEDS and NEEAP both have dedicated sections to finance. Implementation of these policy documents should be complemented and enhanced by a broader policy framework in Georgia, such as on investment promotion and facilitation, capital market development, competition and information base (OECD, 2015; OECD-IEA-ITF-NEA, 2015). Indeed, the government of Georgia plans to significantly raise public investment, starting in 2017 with a focus on road, energy and seaport infrastructure, among others. Failure to mainstream climate and green growth consideration into such public investment will risk locking in the high GHG emissions from infrastructure over the coming decades. (Chapter 4.1.)

Ensuring coherence among a dozen climate- and green growth-related strategic policy documents at the national and sub-national levels will be crucial. Such policy coherence can help build confidence among Georgian stakeholders, in both public and private sectors, to direct their financial resources to climate action. Better coherence will also help the government of Georgia avoid inefficiency and unexpected obstacles. It can also reduce confusion among relevant stakeholders in implementation of strategic measures in those documents. Use of the MARKAL Georgia Model for LEDS and NEEAP has already achieved some built-in coherence. On the other hand, overlaps exist in sectoral coverages between these policy documents. This implies a potential risk of lack, or insufficient level, of coherence among these key strategy documents (Chapter 3.2.).

Financing climate action is needed at both national and municipal levels. Municipalities (including large cities such as Tbilisi and Batumi) face severe financial constraints to improve environmental quality and efficiency of their public infrastructure such as transport and public buildings. Proper implementation and enforcement of the sub-national level policies and mobilisation of necessary finance are critically important. This would help achieve the national targets on climate change and green growth. National-level strategies should also function as an umbrella for sub-national level strategies. No governmental body co-ordinates the different sub-national level policy frameworks across the country. Some Georgian municipalities and development co-operation partners are facilitating investment projects such as the Municipal Project Support Facility (MPSF), the European Bank for Reconstruction and Development's Green City Framework and the Asian Development Bank's Tbilisi Sustainable Urban Transport Programme (Box 3.1. in Chapter 3).

The transport sector is the one of the biggest emitters of Georgia's GHG and air pollutants in urban areas. While there are sub-national level activities as in Tbilisi and Batumi, a national-level strategy on sustainable transport system is in development (UNDP Georgia, 2017). There is no Ministry of Transport, but a division under the Ministry of Economy and Sustainable Development is responsible for inter-city or inter-municipality transport.

Create demand for climate-related activities

Creating demand for investment in climate action relies on a strong and stable policy signal, reasonably stringent environmental regulations and their enforcement, and effective communication to, and engagement with, stakeholders. Georgian enterprises, from small- to large-sized, consider stricter environmental policies to be the most important lever to influence investment decisions e.g. resource efficiency and cleaner production measures (Chorgolashvili, 2017). On the contrary, Georgia is the only country in the Eastern Europe, the Caucasus and Central Asia (EECCA) region, except Turkmenistan, that does not have a quantitative target on renewable energy or energy-efficiency measures as of July 2017. NEEAP is expected to fill this gap by introducing, for instance, energy-efficiency targets and specific measures to achieve them (e.g. energy audit and labelling). The government is developing a national-level renewable energy action plan in light of Georgia's compliance with the Energy Community acquis (Chapters 3.2 to 3.4).

Preferential policy measures (e.g. PPAs and value-added tax exemptions) for hydropower and its untapped potential have successfully enhanced hydropower project development in Georgia. Yet these positive policies may have made it more challenging to draw private investors' attention to "non-hydro" renewable energy projects. Differentiated tariff policies between hydropower and other types of renewable energy (e.g. higher tariffs for wind, solar and geothermal than for hydropower) could ensure a "level-playing field" between different energy sources. Moreover, attractive short-term lending opportunities, such as retail banking (rather than corporate banking) often exacerbate a shortage of long-term capital that could be mobilised to finance climate action in Georgia. These opportunities are certainly positive for economic growth. However, they make it more challenging to increase profiles of long-term investment in corporate banking and "non-hydro" renewable energy.

Further rationalising energy prices in Georgia will greatly help mobilise finance for energy-efficiency measures and smaller-scale renewable projects. These projects, such as energy efficiency at industrial facilities and decentralised solar power at households, have been largely economically unattractive to date (GoG, 2016). The Georgian government has taken steps to increase tax rates on certain fossil fuels (e.g. amendments to the Tax Code in 2017). Still, energy prices remain low. This is mainly due to both the low cost of domestic electricity generation, especially from large-scale hydropower, and subsidy for natural gas used for supplying electricity and heat (IEA, 2015; Pavlenishivili and Biermann, 2016; Singh, et al., 2016; OECD, forthcoming). See also Chapter 3.5.

As many other countries, reforms of energy subsidies have been socially and politically sensitive in Georgia. Energy subsidies should be means-tested and well targeted only for low-income households. Indeed, energy subsidies in Georgia aim to protect socially vulnerable groups from the impact of increases in electricity and natural gas tariffs (hence called "social gas"). Its level is relatively low (1.4% of GDP in 2014) compared to other Eastern Europe and Caucasus countries (OECD, forthcoming). Nonetheless, energy prices do not reflect the full cost of carbon emissions. This has presumably contributed to an increase in natural gas, oil and coal use to meet the country's growing total primary energy supply over the past few years – from 53-72% over 2004-14). See also Chapter 3.5.

An increasing number of countries have overcome the political obstacles to subsidy reforms, including developing nations such as India, Indonesia and Peru (OECD, 2017a). Successful reforms generally have several features. These include data on the monetary value of the subsidies; their distribution across beneficiaries; and analysis of how energy-related services, air quality and/or GHG emissions could be improved when prices better reflect costs (OECD, 2017a). An energy subsidy inventory in Georgia, developed by the OECD (forthcoming), can help Georgia pursue further reforms to energy subsidies.

"Greening" Georgia's public procurement system can help create demand for investment in low-emission goods and services, and trigger industrial and business model innovation (OECD, 2017a). Georgia's State Procurement Agency can consider integrating environmental and energy performance criteria into the Law on Public Procurement. Georgia's procurement system works well to ensure competitive public tendering, but does not adequately consider lifetime environmental or energy performance of goods and services (OECD, 2016b; Singh, et al., 2016). The ratio of the government's expenditures for purchases of goods and services to GDP accounts for 18.4% (World Bank, 2017d). How the government spends this money can have a considerable impact on the dissemination of products and services (Baron, 2016). See also Chapter 3.6.

Improve the capital market and other enabling conditions to meet investment demand

Developing a well-functioning capital market has great potential to help diversify financial channels. It can also lower investment costs and complement bank lending. In so doing, it can enhance the flow of capital in Georgia, including for climate action, over time (MoESD, 2016; OECD, 2017a, 2017b). The role of the capital market is modest in Georgia. Commercial banks held 91.9% of financial sector assets in 2015, followed by microfinance institutions and credit unions (5.9%) (MoESD, 2016). Public and private sectors have provided equity investments, particularly to large-scale renewable energy projects such as hydropower. They have invested less in smaller-scale, non-hydro renewables and energy-efficiency projects (see Chapter 4.1. for further detail). Non-bank financing channels, such as lease, vendor credits and private-sector energy service companies, are limited as financial channels for energy efficiency in Georgia. However, these channels could improve risk-return profiles of energy-efficiency activities and projects (Chernyavskay and van Waveren Horgervorst, 2017).

Georgia is making progress in developing its financial markets (e.g. securities market, money market and payment system). These can offer an opportunity to develop a comprehensive financial sector that is also conducive to green finance mobilisation. Markets related to climate, or green growth, have yet to become part of this work. However, actors working on financial market development have shown growing interest in this issue at several forums in Georgia (e.g. OECD, 2017d; Van Bilsen, 2017). The government and the National Bank of Georgia have been reviewing legal frameworks relating to financial sector regulations. This can provide a basis for examining where climate risks could be "mainstreamed" into the individual menus of financial market reform in the short- and long-run. Moreover, regardless of an explicit green mandate in the reform of the Georgian capital market, improving the market will have direct and indirect implications for future green finance mobilisation (Chapter 5.1.2).

Interest in green bonds is increasing in Georgia, although none has been issued to date (Van Bilsen, 2017). Some major challenges still exist, such as scalability of projects and Georgia's nascent bond market. The government of Georgia, in collaboration with the National Bank of Georgia, would also need to develop its green bond standard or adopt ones developed by other institutions or countries. Analysis shows that, globally, bond financing for renewables, energy efficiency and low-carbon vehicles could reach USD 620-720 billion per year by 2035 from USD 95 billion in 2016 (OECD, 2017b). Bilateral and multilateral development finance institutions could support a demonstration issuance of green bonds in Georgia by, for instance, purchasing green bonds through a cornerstone investment fund (IFC, 2017). See Chapter 4.2.

Microfinance institutions, institutional investors and non-financial sector corporations could play a greater role in financial flows to climate action in Georgia. Some microfinance institutions (e.g. MFO Crystal) and commercial banks that primarily target SMEs (e.g. JSC ProCredit Bank) are making progress in designing and providing loans to energy-efficiency activities and smaller-scale, often decentralised, renewable energy facilities. Microfinance is, however, likely to need concessional financing to lower its high interest rates. Lower rates are needed because energy-efficiency activities and decentralised renewable energy typically have long payback periods and greater levels of technical uncertainty. The Dutch Development Bank, FMO, started to work with MFO Crystal on a green microfinance programme in 2017 (Chapter 4.2.)

Georgia is also reforming its pension system (Schwarz et al., 2016; Paresishvili, 2017). This might be a future source of funding for climate-related projects through direct investment or purchase of green bonds. The accumulation of pension fund assets is expected to increase from GEL 313 million (USD 128.8 million) in 2018 to GEL 29.7 billion (USD 12.2 billion) in 2035 (Paresishvili, 2017). However, further clarity is needed whether such climate-related projects or green bonds can be an eligible asset class for Georgian pension funds (Chapter 4.2).

There is neither a national development bank nor a green investment bank in Georgia. However, investors, commercial banks and corporations active in Georgia could benefit from such a national funding entity to scale up their investments in climate action. LEDS and NEEAP have separately proposed options to set up a public entity with a specific mandate on green finance. It might deliver direct investment in or risk mitigation instruments, or both, to climate-related projects.

There is further need to review public financing entities and mechanisms. A comprehensive approach is required to mobilise green finance to implement the NDC, LEDS, NEEAP, NAMAs, SEAPs and other key policy documents. Such an approach should also avoid the fragmentation of the financial mechanisms and crowding-out of potential private-sector finance. Further, it should provide investment and/or risk mitigation instruments to underserved sectors (e.g. transport sector and SMEs) and activities (e.g. energy efficiency and other renewable energy than hydropower).

Establishing a green bank (or fund) may be an idea worth exploring (Park, 2017; Winrock and Remissia, 2017). Yet it might also be sensible to strengthen the functions and/or scale of an existing state fund or entity to build greater support for "green" aspects within their own mandates. Such entities could include JSC Partnership Fund, JSC Georgian Energy Development Fund (GEDF), Enterprise Georgia and the Municipal Development Fund. This process could be supported by a review of national financial institutions. It should assess expenditure on climate-related activities and their needs related to information, capacities and institutional arrangements. See also Chapter 5.1.3.

A comprehensive stocktaking and review of risk mitigation instruments that are available or missing in the country can be useful. A range of domestic and international providers of public finance has deployed various risk mitigation instruments for climate action in Georgia, such as credit enhancement mechanisms and direct public investment. Examples include fixed tariffs agreed by the government for renewable energy, (partial) credit guarantees, fund seeding through sovereign funds (e.g. the GEDF and the Partnership Fund) and cornerstone stake investment (e.g. GEEREF) (see also Table 5.3 in Chapter 5.1.). Nevertheless, there is still great demand for low-cost financing, and Georgia's fiscal space is limited. Thus, making efficient use of available risk mitigation instruments is important. Similarly, it is critical to identify important risks not adequately covered in the country. Both can improve the risk-return profiles of climate-related projects. See also Chapter 5.1.3.

Open, competitive and unbundled electricity markets, if designed properly, create more space for renewable energy in developing countries, including Georgia (OECD, 2015). In this regard, the government should fully seize opportunities that stem from Georgia's new status as a Contracting Party to the Treaty establishing the Energy Community (Energy Community Treaty) to promote further renewable energy and energy efficiency. Georgia has a well-functioning power sector in general. However, multiple organisations have concluded that creating a more competitive and transparent electricity market remains a critical challenge (ADB, 2015; Kochladz et al., 2015; Energy Community Secretariat, 2017). See Chapter 5.2.

On the other hand, state-owned enterprises in the energy sector, such as the Electricity System Commercial Operator (ESCO), the Georgian State Electrosystem (GSE), and the Energotrans LLC can also promote the government's green growth agenda. This agenda could be pushed, for instance, through preferential financing and influencing policy via the boards of the entities (Prag and Röttgers, 2017). NEEAP also proposes loss reduction in electricity transmission networks and grid integration of new generation by GSE and modernisation of railways by the Georgian Railways, among others (NEEAP Expert Team, 2017). However, promotion of green growth through state-owned entities must not be used to justify an uncompetitive energy market (Chapter 5.2).

To bridge the information gap, the government of Georgia could establish, or help establish, a central data depository. This would collect, collate and maintain information on, for example, loan-level data, performance track records of investment projects, and technologies and hydro-meteorological data. Georgia's first Biennial Update Report (submitted to UNFCCC) describes the lack of data on climate change-related information as chaotic, dispersed, inaccurate, outdated and unreliable. It is thus one of the biggest obstacles to climate change action in Georgia (GoG, 2016). Better understanding among potential borrowers about energy-efficiency technologies and their cost-benefit profiles could have expedited disbursement of credit for renewable energy and energy efficiency. A range of countries are also setting up learning networks and platforms to improve information flows, raise awareness of benefits from green investment and good national and international practices, and enhance analytical capabilities. See also Chapter 5.3.

Notes

1. Based on the poverty line of USD 2.5 per day purchasing power parity (PPP).
2. During the drafting period of this report, LEDS and NEEAP were still under review by the government. Thus, this report referred to the draft documents for LEDS and NEEAP prepared by Winrock International and Sustainable Development Center Remissia (for LEDS) and the NEEAP Expert Team (for NEEAP).

References

ADB (2015), *Assessment of Power Sector Reforms in Asia: Experience of Georgia, Sri Lanka and Vietnam – Synthesis Report*, Asian Development Bank (ADB), Mandaluyong City, Philippines, https://www.adb.org/documents/assessment-power-sector-reforms-asia-synthesis.

Baron, R. (2016), *The Role of Public Procurement in Low-carbon Innovation*, Background paper for the 33rd Round Table on Sustainable Development, 12-13 April 2016, OECD, Paris, https://www.oecd.org/sd-roundtable/papersandpublications/The%20Role%20of%20Public%20Procurement%20in%20Low-carbon%20Innovation.pdf.

Chernyavskay, T. and M. van Waveren Horgervorst (2017), "Financing RECP measures at SMEs: An overlooked opportunity", presentation at International Conference: Unlocking Private Finance for Energy Efficiency and Greener, Low-Carbon Growth in the Eastern Partnership and Central Asia Countries, Brussels, 30 June 2017, https://www.slideshare.net/OECD_ENV/session-4-presentation-by-tatiana-chernyavskaya-and-marko-van-waveren-unido.

Chorgolashvili, A. (2017), "Research about opportunities and barriers to promote RECP financing in Georgia", presentation to OECD workshop on green finance mobilisation in Georgia, Tbilisi, 22-23 June 2017, https://www.slideshare.net/OECD_ENV/session-6-presentation-by-unido (accessed 9 October 2017).

Copenhagen Centre on Energy Efficiency (2017), *Energy Efficiency Brief: Tbilisi, Georgia*, Copenhagen Centre on Energy Efficiency, http://kms.energyefficiencycentre.org/publication-report/energy-efficiency-brief-tbilisi-georgia.

Covenant of Mayors (2017), "Covenant of Mayors – Signatories", webpage, www.covenantofmayors.eu/about/about/signatories_en.html?commitments2=1&commitments3=1&commitments1=1 (accessed 9 June 2017).

EBRD (2015), "Gori Wind Power Plant, Project Support Document", webpage, European Bank for Reconstruction and Development, London www.ebrd.com/work-with-us/projects/psd/gori-wind.html (accessed 28 July 2017).

EIB (2016), *Georgia: Neighbourhood SME Financing*, European Investment Bank, Luxembourg, www.eib.org/attachments/efs/economic_report_neighbourhood_sme_financing_georgia_en.pdf.

Energy Community Secretariat (2017), *Energy Governance in Georgia, Report on Compliance with the Energy Community Acquis*, Energy Community Secretariat, Vienna, www.euneighbours.eu/sites/default/files/publications/2017-08/ECS_Georgia_Report_082017.pdf.

EU4Business (2017), *Investing in SMEs in the Eastern Partnership Countries: Georgia Country Report*, EU4Business, Belgium, http://eu4business.com/files/medias/country_report_georgia.pdf.

GEDF (2017), "Georgian Energy Development Fund announces Selection of Investor for development of Zestaponi WPP Project", webpage, http://gedf.com.ge/en/georgian-energy-development-fund-announces-selection-of-investor-for-devepolment-of-zestaponi-wpp-project/ (accessed 18 August 2017).

GoG (2016), *First Biennial Update Report on Climate Change*, Government of Georgia, Tbilisi http://unfccc.int/files/national_reports/non-annex_i_parties/ica/application/pdf/first_bur_-_georgia.pdf.

GoG (2015a), *Georgia's Intended Nationally Determined Contribution*, Government of Georgia, Tbilisi, http://www4.unfccc.int/submissions/INDC/Published%20Documents/Georgia/1/INDC_of_Georgia.pdf.

GoG (2015b), *Third National Communication of Georgia to the UN Framework Convention on Climate Change (UNFCCC)*, Government of Georgia, Tbilisi, www.ge.undp.org/content/georgia/en/home/library/environment_energy/third-national-communication-of-georgia-to-the-un-framework-conv0/.

GoG (2014), *Social-economic Development Strategy of Georgia: GEORGIA 2020*, Government of Georgia, Tbilisi, https://policy.asiapacificenergy.org/sites/default/files/Georgia%202020_ENG.pdf.

IEA (2017), *World Energy Balances of non-OECD Countries 2015*, OECD Publishing, Paris, https://www.iea.org/statistics/statisticssearch/report/?country=Georgia&product=balances.

IEA (2015), *Energy Policies Beyond IEA Countries: Caspian and Black Sea Regions 2015*, OECD Publishing, Paris, http://dx.doi.org/10.1787/9789264228719-en.

IFC (2017), "IFC, Amundi to create world's largest green-bond fund dedicated to emerging markets", *Press Release*, 21 April 2017, International Finance Corporation, Washington, DC, https://ifcextapps.ifc.org/IFCExt/pressroom/IFCPressRoom.nsf/0/2CC3EDA1AE8B9B558525810900546887 (accessed 9 October 2017).

IMF (2017) "Georgia : Request for extended arrangement under the Extended Fund Facility and cancellation of stand-by arrangement-press release; staff report; and statement by the Executive Director for Georgia", *Country Report*, No. 17/97, International Monetary Fund, Washington, DC, https://www.imf.org/en/Publications/CR/Issues/2017/04/13/Georgia-Request-for-Extended-Arrangement-Under-the-Extended-Fund-Facility-and-Cancellation-44834.

Kochladz, M. et al. (2015), *Georgia and European Energy Community – The Challenges of EU Integration*, Green Alternative, Tbilisi, https://greenalt.org/wp-content/uploads/2015/06/Georgia_and_European_Energy_Community.pdf.

McNicoll, L. and R. Jachnik (2017), *The "Investor Perspective" for Estimating Publicly-mobilised Private Finance for Climate Action: Methodological Proposal and Case Studies*, Researchers Collaborative, OECD Publishing, Paris, https://www.oecd.org/env/researchcollaborative.

Ministry of Energy (2017), *More Renewables and Improved Energy Efficiency: Energy Policy in Georgia*, Ministry of Energy of Georgia, Tbilisi, https://www.unece.org/fileadmin/DAM/env/documents/2017/WAT/04Apr_11_5SC/GE_5SC_Arabidze_EN.pdf.

MoESD (2016), *Capital Market Development Strategy*, Ministry of Economy and Sustainable Development with the Ministry of Finance and the National Bank of Georgia, Tbilisi.

NEEAP Expert Team (2017), "Draft National Energy Efficiency Action Plan", report commissioned by European Bank for Reconstruction and Development, NEEP Expert Team.

OECD (forthcoming), *Inventory of Energy Subsidies in the EU's Eastern Partnership Countries*, OECD Publishing, Paris.

OECD (2017a), *Investing in Climate, Investing in Growth*, OECD Publishing, Paris, http://dx.doi.org/10.1787/9789264273528-en.

OECD (2017b), *Mobilising Bond Markets for a Low-Carbon Transition*, OECD Publishing, Paris, http://dx.doi.org/10.1787/9789264272323-en.

OECD (2017c), "Green Growth Indicators", *OECD Environment Statistics* (database), http://dx.doi.org/10.1787/data-00665-en (accessed 31 October 2017).

OECD (2017d), *Summary Record of Workshop on Green Finance Mobilisation in Georgia*, www.oecd.org/environment/outreach/Summary%20record_OECD-MoENRP%20Green%20Finance%20Mobilisation%20Workshop%20(Tbilisi)%2022-23.07.2017.pdf.

OECD (2016a), *Responsible Business Conduct in Georgia*, OECD Publishing, Paris, www.oecd.org/countries/georgia/RBC-in-Georgia-2016.pdf.

OECD (2016b), *Promoting Better Environmental Performance of SMEs: Georgia*, www.oecd.org/env/outreach/Georgia%20pilot%20project%20report%20final%20EN.pdf.

OECD (2015), *Policy Guidance for Investment in Clean Energy Infrastructure: Expanding Access to Clean Energy for Green Growth and Development*, OECD Publishing, Paris, http://dx.doi.org/10.1787/9789264212664-en.

OECD-IEA-ITF-NEA (2015), *Aligning Policies for a Low-carbon Economy*, OECD Publishing, Paris, http://dx.doi.org/10.1787/9789264233294-en.

Paresishvili, G. (2017), *Georgian Stock Exchange: Georgian Capital Market Development*, https://www.saras.gov.ge/Content/files/GSE-Capital-Market-Development-FINAL-ENG-19.06.17.pdf (accessed 31 October 2017).

Park, L. (2017), "Creation of Green Banks", presentation at Green Climate Fund workshop, presentation to OECD workshop on green finance mobilisation in Georgia, Tbilisi, 22-23 June 2017, https://www.slideshare.net/OECD_ENV/session-5-presentation-by-green-climate-fund (accessed 9 October 2017).

Partnership Fund (14 June 2016), "Partnership Fund launches Ytong energy efficient block factory project", JSC Partnership Fund News and Media blog, www.fund.ge/eng/view_news/736.

Pavlenishivili, L. and F. Biermann (10 May 2016), "No price caps in the electricity wholesale market!", The Financial Opinion and Blogs, https://www.finchannel.com/opinion/57148-no-price-caps-in-the-electricity-wholesale-market (accessed 9 October 2017).

Prag, A. and D. Röttgers (2017), *State-Owned Enterprises and the Low-Carbon Transition*, OECD Publishing, Paris.

Singh, J. et al. (2016), *Energy Efficiency Financing Option Papers for Georgia*, World Bank, Washington, DC, http://documents.worldbank.org/curated/en/825761475845097689/Energy-efficiency-financing-option-papers-for-Georgia.

UNDP Georgia (2017), "Georgia to develop national strategy of sustainable urban transport | UNDP in Georgia", *Press Release*, 28 February 2017, United Nations Development Programme, Tbilisi, Georgia, www.ge.undp.org/content/georgia/en/home/presscenter/pressreleases/2017/02/28/georgia-will-develop-national-strategy-of-sustainable-urban-transport-.html (accessed 9 October 2017).

UNECE (2016), *Third Environmental Performance Reviews of Georgia*, United Nations Economic Commission for Europe (UNECE), Geneva, https://www.unece.org/fileadmin/DAM/env/epr/epr_studies/ECE_CEP_177.pdf.

Van Bilsen, J. (16 January 2017), "Green Bond Market in Georgia – a Growing Opportunity" Georgia Today on the Web News blog, http://georgiatoday.ge/news/5609/Green-Bond-Market-in-Georgia-%E2%80%93-a-Growing-Opportunity (accessed 9 October 2017).

Schwarz, A. et al. (2016), "Pension reform in Georgia", www.economy.ge/uploads/meniu_publikaciebi/ouer/msoplio_bankis_prezentacia.pdf (acessed 30 October 2017).

Winrock and Remmisia (2017), "Georgia Low Emission Development Strategy Draft Report", commissioned by USAID-funded EC-LEDS Clean Energy Program, Winrock International and Sustainable Development Center, Remissia, Tbilisi.

World Bank (2017a) *Trade in Transition: Europe and Central Asia Economic Update*, World Bank Group, Washington, DC, www.worldbank.org/en/region/eca/publication/europe-and-central-asia-economic-update.

World Bank (2017b) *Georgia – Private Sector Competitiveness Development Policy Operation,* World Bank, Washington, DC, http://documents.worldbank.org/curated/en/478801501725663367/pdf/Georgia-Private-Sector-Competitiveness-PD-07112017.pdf.

World Bank (2017d), *World Development Indicators,* World Bank Group, http://wdi.worldbank.org/tables (accessed 31 October 2017).

Chapter 2

Investment needs for achieving Georgia's climate targets

This chapter takes stock of investment needs to achieve Georgia's climate targets. The Georgian government and its development co-operation partners have estimated investment needs for the country's climate action, but information is often fragmented in different policy documents. Thus this chapter reviews several publicly available information sources and attempts an overview of the needs for finance towards 2030. It highlights the National Energy Efficiency Action Plan, the Low Emission Development Strategy, the Nationally Determined Contribution, among others.

An analysis of Georgia's strategic policy documents reaffirms that massive investment will be needed to achieve the country's targets on climate change and green growth agendas. It is a challenging task to estimate investment needs for climate action to achieve the given targets such as in the nationally determined contribution (NDC). Georgia, like many other countries, has not yet determined the total volume of national-level investment needs until 2030. In general, it remains technically demanding to define what to count as finance for climate action, estimate investment needs (both gross and incremental) precisely, define timeframes, prioritise sectors and projects, and identify specific financial sources, among others.

Stocktaking of investment needs for climate action in Georgia

Figure 2.1. intends to take stock of investment needs in light of Georgia's climate-related targets under the NDC and the Low Emission Development Strategy (LEDS). The sectors include energy use (e.g. buildings and industry); energy supply (generation and distribution); transport; land use, land-use change and forestry (LULUCF); non-energy related greenhouse gas (GHG) emissions (e.g. agriculture, industrial process and waste) and climate change adaptation. The stocktaking is based on the policy documents and other publicly available information. Information in Figure 2.1. is by no means sufficient to obtain a complete picture of financial needs towards 2030. Methodologies for estimates might have been different across the documents.

Various policy documents in Georgia offer several useful, yet slightly fragmented, information on potential costs of climate action in the country. For instance, LEDS estimates long-term investment needs for nearly 40 measures in various sectors. Meanwhile, several other measures, such as policy reforms, are still to be calculated (Winrock and Remmisia, 2017). The National Energy Efficiency Action Plan (NEEAP) shows that the total gross financial needs for energy efficiency under NEEAP are expected to be approximately USD 8.3 billion from 2017 to 2030. NEEAP contains the cost estimates of seven thematic measures: buildings, industry, transport, energy supply and demand sectors, and horizontal measures (NEEAP Expert Team, 2017).

The estimated costs of developing renewable energy projects, which appear in some policy documents, still seem to require further scrutiny especially for other sources than hydropower. Georgia's third National Communication to the UN Framework Convention on Climate Change (UNFCCC) reveals insights about the continued expansion of hydropower development. A cumulative additional capacity of 2 601 MW by 2030 would cost about USD 2.4 billion for 2017-30 (GoG, 2015a). In terms of wind and solar energy, the estimates included in Figure 2.1 only show information drawn from several documents prepared by the government and financial institutions. These include the Ministry of Energy, the Georgian Energy Development Fund (GEDF) and the European Bank for Reconstruction and Development (EBRD) (EBRD, 2015; Khaindrava, 2017; Ministry of Energy, 2017). Therefore, these estimates do not consider future financial needs for projects that may be developed by 2030, but have not been committed or considered yet.

The NDC shows costs for adaptation measures, such as climate-resilient coastal infrastructure, water management, and agriculture and forest management. These would amount to between USD 1.5-2.0 billion over 2021-30 (GoG, 2015). The estimate was based on expert judgement, but no background information is available in the NDC or any other policy documents.

Figure 2.1. **Stocktaking of long-term investment needs (USD million)**

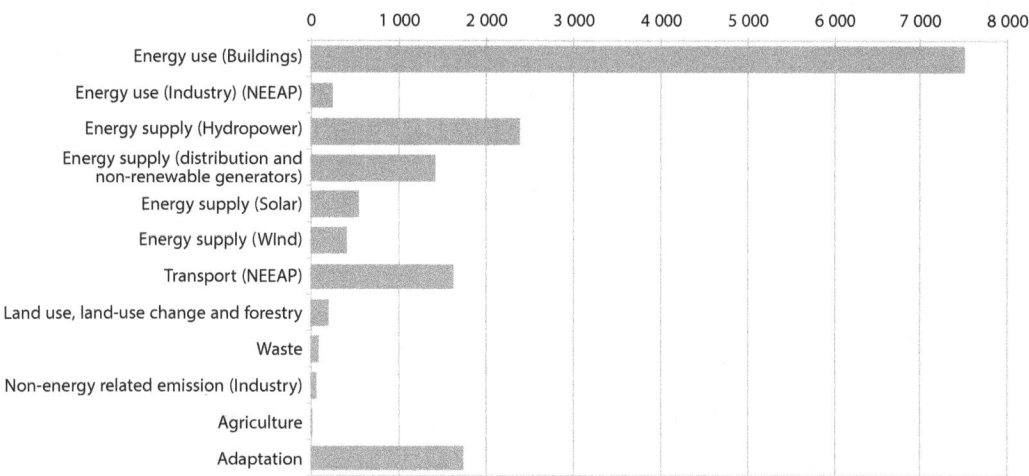

Notes: 1. Cost estimate methodologies may differ among the information sources. Therefore, this figure does not aggregate the numbers at the national level.

2. Estimates for energy use in the industry and transport sectors are derived from NEEAP. The estimate for adaptation cost is based on the figure included in the NDC. The estimate for hydropower plants is derived from the Third National Communication of Georgia. The rest comes from LEDS.

Source: Author's calculations, based on GoG (2015a, 2015b), GEDF (2017), NEEAP Expert Team (2017) and Winrock and Remmisia (2017).

The Ministry of Energy (2017) emphasises the importance of further solar and wind energy projects and outlines potential projects. However, there has not been any quantitative target on renewable energy introduction at the national level or a clear project pipeline to date. The absence of a quantitative target makes it more challenging to provide a credible prospect of investment needs for such renewable energy plants. In one estimate, ongoing and potential renewable energy projects include 146 power plants (mostly hydropower). They have a projected total installed capacity of 5 358 MW, which would require investments of approximately USD 8.8 billion (Energy Community Secretariat, 2017).

To complement Figure 2.1, Table 2.1 outlines several "non-hydro" renewable projects, either implemented or planned. This implies possible further increases in investment needs for renewables beyond those in Figure 2.1. For instance, in 2016, the first Georgian wind power plant, Qartli Wind Farm (20 MW), began operation. It is forecasted to generate 88.0 GWh of electricity annually. The Georgian Energy Development Fund is also developing the larger Zestafoni Wind Power Plant Project, with an expected cost of USD 227 million (Khaindrava, 2017). JSC Caucasian Solar Company is studying the feasibility of solar energy projects that, if pursued, would be completed in 2018. The total expected installed capacity of these potential projects would reach 500 MW and cost around USD 490 million (Ministry of Energy, 2017).

Table 2.1. **Examples of renewable energy projects in Georgia, excluding hydropower**

Type	Main actors	Description	Status as of July 2017
Wind	GEDF, GOGC, EBRD, etc.	WPP owned by Qartli Wind Farm LLC, owned by GEDF and JSC Georgian Oil and Gas Corporation (GOGC) as of August 2017, while its shares plan to be sold through the Georgian Stock Exchange	Installed
	GEDF and Calik Enerji Sanayi ve Ticaret A.S	Nigoza WPP (installed capacity of 40 MW in Shida Kartli region)	Planned
	GEDF and Calik Enerji Sanayi ve Ticaret A.S	WPP (a total installed capacity of 120 MW) in the Imereti districts	Planned
	GEDF	GEDF invited investors to express interest in joint development of another WPP in Zestaponi, with an estimated installed capacity of 150 MW	Planned
	GEDF	GEDF conducts feasibility study for Qartli Wind Farm Phase 2 with an estimated installed capacity of 150 MW	Planned
Solar	Tbilisi International Airport	316 KW Solar PV installation	Installed
	Ilia State University	35 KW Solar PV installations	Installed
	JSC Caucasus Solar Company	Feasibility studies for Akhaltsikhe Solar Power Plants 1 and 2, Gardabani Solar Power Plants 1 and 2, Gldani Solar Power Plant, Algeta Solar Power Plant, Kaspi Solar Power Plant, Marneuli Solar Power Plant, Saakadze Solar Power Plant and Ksani Solar Power Plant.	(Under feasibility study)
	GEDF	A solar power plant in Udabno, Kakheti region, with an estimated installed capacity of 5 MW.	Planned

EBRD: European Bank for Reconstruction and Development; **GEDF**: Georgian Energy Development Fund; **GOGC**: Georgian Oil and Gas Corporation; **WPP**: wind power plants.

Source: Author's analysis based on EBRD (2015), Khaindrava (2017) and Ministry of Energy (2017).

Capital sources to meet the needs: An example from NEEAP

Various sources, including private and public sectors and households, should be used to meet financial needs for climate action in Georgia. In Figure 2.2, for example, cost estimates under NEEAP divide energy efficiency costs by source. It shows that a substantial share of the finance for energy efficiency should come from domestic public sources including state-owned entities (more than 40%), as well as from domestic and international private sectors.

These state-owned entities include JSC Georgian State Electrosystem (GSE), JSC Georgian Railway and JSC Georgian Oil and Gas Corporation (GOGC),[1] which are expected to invest in or channel finance for energy-efficient infrastructure. For instance, NEEAP proposes loss reduction in electricity transmission networks and grid integration of new generation by GSE; modernisation of railways by the Georgian Railways; and replacement of old thermal power plants with new technologies by GOGC (NEEAP Expert Team, 2017).

NEEAP also expects private sector entities and households to provide nearly 30% of finance. This contribution increases to 60% of total estimated investment needs if it includes finance to replace passenger transport with hybrid and electric vehicles. NEEAP does not break down the private-sector investment in terms of domestic and international sources. Chapter 4 reviews currently and potentially available financial channels for climate action in Georgia, including those from private sector sources.

Figure 2.2. **Expected financial sources for energy-efficiency measures in NEEAP for 2017-30**

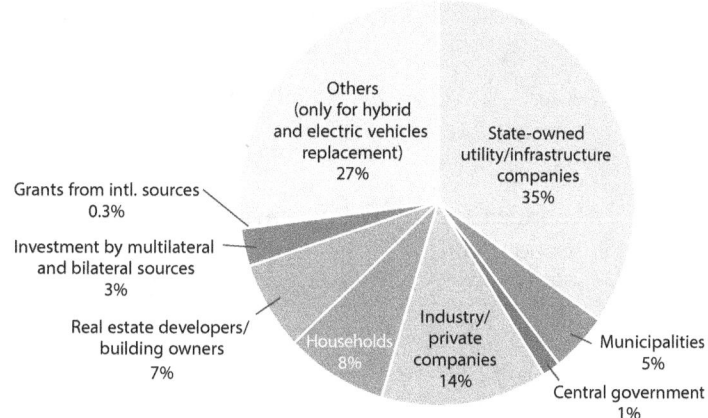

Notes: 1. The original estimates were made in euros. The exchange rate applied is USD 1 = EUR 0.904 according to OECD (2017), Exchange rates (indicator), http://dx.doi.org/10.1787/037ed317-en (accessed 14 August 2017).

2. "State-owned utility/infrastructure companies" include JSC Georgian State Electrosystem, JSC Georgian Railway and JSC Georgian Oil and Gas Corporation.

Source: Author's calculations based on NEEAP Expert Team (2017).

Note

1. These companies are owned by JSC Partnership Fund, a national fund wholly owned by the Georgian government. Thus they are indirectly owned by the state.

References

EBRD (2015), "Gori Wind Power Plant, Project Support Document", webpage, www.ebrd.com/work-with-us/projects/psd/gori-wind.html (accessed 28 July 2017).

Energy Community Secretariat (2017), *Energy Governance in Georgia, Report on Compliance with the Energy Community Acquis*, www.euneighbours.eu/sites/default/files/publications/2017-08/ECS_Georgia_Report_082017.pdf.

GEDF (2017), *Georgian Energy Development Fund announces Selection of Investor for development of Zestaponi WPP Project | GEDF*, Georgian Energy Development Fund, Tbilisi, http://gedf.com.ge/en/georgian-energy-development-fund-announces-selection-of-investor-for-devepolment-of-zestaponi-wpp-project/.

GoG (2016), *First Biennial Update Report on Climate Change*, Government of Georgia, Tbilisi, http://unfccc.int/files/national_reports/non-annex_i_parties/ica/application/pdf/first_bur_-_georgia.pdf.

GoG (2015a), *Third National Communication of Georgia to the UN Framework Convention on Climate Change (UNFCCC)*, Government of Georgia, Tbilisi, www.ge.undp.org/content/georgia/en/home/library/environment_energy/third-national-communication-of-georgia-to-the-un-framework-conv0/.

GoG (2015b), *Georgia's Intended Nationally Determined Contribution*, Government of Georgia, Tbilisi, http://www4.unfccc.int/submissions/INDC/Published%20Documents/Georgia/1/INDC_of_Georgia.pdf.

Khaindrava, N. (2017), "Georgian Energy Development Fund", presentation at workshop on green finance mobilisation, Tbilisi, 22 June 2017, https://www.slideshare.net/OECD_ENV/session-3-presentation-by-georgian-development-fund. (accessed 28 October 2017).

Ministry of Energy (2017), *More Renewables and Improved Energy Efficiency: Energy Policy in Georgia*, Ministry of Energy, Tbilisi, https://www.unece.org/fileadmin/DAM/env/documents/2017/WAT/04Apr_11_5SC/GE_5SC_Arabidze_EN.pdf.

NEEAP Expert Team (2017), *Draft National Energy Efficiency Action Plan*, report commissioned by European Bank for Reconstruction and Development, London.

Winrock and Remmisia (2017), "Georgia Low Emission Development Strategy Draft Report", commissioned by the USAID-funded EC-LEDS Clean Energy Program, Winrock International and Sustainable Development Center, Remissia, Tbilisi.

Chapter 3

Creating investment needs: Overview of climate policies in Georgia

Strong and stable climate policies are essential to create demand for investment in climate action in Georgia. Climate policies and regulations that directly affect business opportunities, costs, risk and returns on investment are often uncertain. Indeed, this is one of the most frequently cited barriers to scaling up finance for climate action in Georgia and elsewhere in the world. This chapter provides a brief overview of the country's nationally determined contribution (NDC) and two key strategic policy documents: the Low Emission Development Strategy (LEDS) and the National Energy Efficiency Action Plan (NEEAP). It also touches upon other strategic policy documents related to climate change mitigation in Georgia.

Outline of Georgia's nationally determined contribution

With certain fluctuation, Georgia's greenhouse gas (GHG) emissions have increased 3.5% annually on average between 2004 and 2013 (Figure 3.1). The trend correlates with the economy: GHG emissions increased between 2004 and 2007, when economic growth reached its peak. Emissions subsequently declined for several reasons. These include the recession from the global economic crisis that started in 2008, the war in the same year and the increase of hydropower in the electricity generation sector over those years. Since 2011, GHG emissions have increased again due to several factors. These include revival of economic growth and a subsequent increase in demand for electricity. Other factors are relatively low precipitation, affecting water resources available for hydropower. Finally, industry increased its consumption of coal (GoG, 2015a).

While Georgia benefits from a substantial amount of water resources for hydropower, the largest share of GHG emissions comes from the energy sector (Figure 3.1). In 2013, GHG emissions from the energy sector amounted to 9.4 million tonnes of carbon dioxide equivalent (MtCO$_2$), which is about 56% of Georgia's total GHG emissions. GHG emissions from the energy sector can be disaggregated as follows: transport (33%), manufacturing industries and construction (21%), gas transmission and distribution (19%) and electricity production (10%) (GoG, 2015a).

Figure 3.1. **GHG emissions trend and NDC targets**

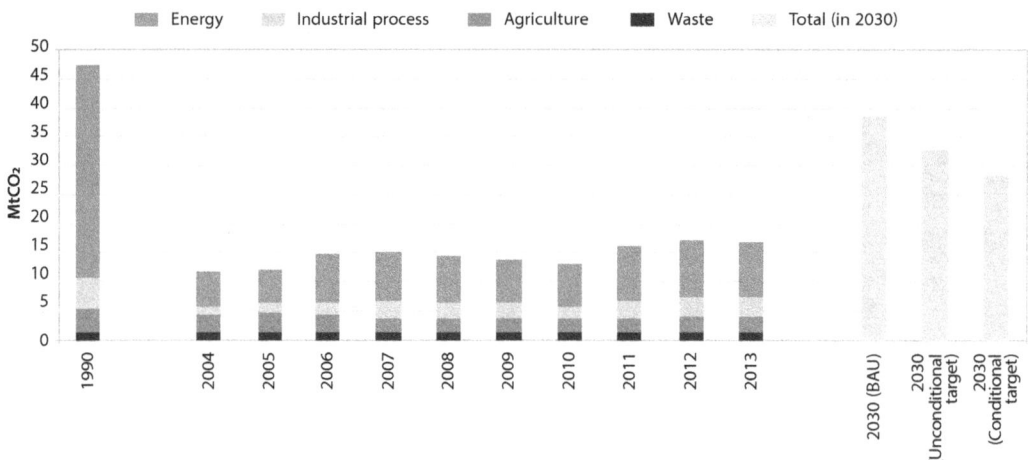

Note: GHG emissions here exclude those from land use, land-use change and forestry (LULUCF).

Source: Author's analysis based on GoG (2016, 2015b).

Georgia's unconditional target under the nationally determined contribution (NDC) is to reduce GHG emissions by 15% below the business as usual (BAU) scenario in 2030 (Figure 3.1, Table 3.1). Assuming international financial support and technology transfer, it has a conditional target to reduce GHG emissions by 25% below BAU in 2030 (GoG, 2015b). In absolute terms, a 15% reduction below BAU means about 32% below the GHG emission in 1990. A 25% reduction below BAU is approximately 41% below the 1990 level. The Ministry of Environment and Natural Resources Protection is also developing a Climate Action Plan. This will act as an NDC implementation plan, and include concrete steps and figures for achieving climate-related targets of the country.

Table 3.1. **Overview of Georgia's nationally determined contribution**

Scope of action	Targets	Priority sectors for mitigation actions
Mitigation	(Unconditional target) To reduce GHG emissions by 15% below the BAU* by 2030	Energy efficiency and renewable energy on both the supply and demand sides
	(Target conditional on international support) To reduce GHG emissions by 25% below the BAU* by 2030	(Same as above)
Adaptation	To improve the country's preparedness and adaptive capacity by developing climate-resilient practices that reduce vulnerability of highly exposed communities.	Agriculture disaster risk management; coastal zone protection
Means of implementation	Quantified needs if any	Description
Finance	(The NDC mentions that the more ambitious target is subject to "technical co-operation, access to low-cost financial resources and technology transfer".)	The NDC does not indicate specific figures of need to be supported by international sources, but indicates that the total adaptation costs would be USD 1.5-2 billion in 2021-30.
Capacity development	(Same as above)	N.A.
Technology Transfer	(Same as above)	Priorities in the needs for international support for technologies transfer: protection of coastal infrastructure; technologies for sustainable water management; sustainable agricultural technologies; and technologies for sustainable forest management.

* BAU: Business as usual.
Source: OECD (2016) based on GoG (2015b).

Georgia's NDC does not systematically indicate the size of finance needed to achieve its GHG emission reduction targets, even for those contingent on international financial and technical support. The NDC mentions the level of adaptation finance needed (USD 15-20 billion over 2021-30). However, there is no information to clarify how these figures have been elicited or any reference to background information that backs the figures.

The adaptation section of the NDC mentions agriculture, disaster risk management and coastal protection against the sea-level rise of the Black Sea as priority areas for Georgia. The NDC also outlines types of technologies for which international support is needed, such as for protection of coastal infrastructure; sustainable water management; sustainable agriculture; and sustainable forest management. Implementation will be further elaborated in the country's national adaptation plan (NAP).

Strategic policy documents on climate action and broader development agenda

Strong and stable policy frameworks are the crucial enabler for any country to create demand for green investment. Georgia is making great progress in policy development on climate and green growth agenda – some at the national level, while others at the sectoral or sub-national level (Table 3.2). Socio-Economic Development Strategy "Georgia 2020" was adopted in 2014 as a national-level, overarching strategy to pursue sustainable and inclusive economic growth towards 2020 and beyond (GoG, 2014). It covers an extensive range of issues, including macroeconomic policy frameworks, competitiveness of the private sector, development of human resources and access to finance. Georgia 2020 also covers climate-related issues such as renewable energy and energy efficiency promotion.

Table 3.2. **Examples of laws and strategic policy documents relating to climate change action in Georgia**

Name	Scope	Status	Note
Nationally Determined Contribution	National	Submitted to UNFCCC in 2015	Communicates Georgia's climate-related targets internationally
Georgia 2020	National	Adopted in 2014	Identifies priorities and problems to be dealt with to achieve long-term, sustainable and inclusive economic growth, including renewable energy and energy efficiency
Main Directions of the State Policy in Energy Sector	National/ Sectoral	Adopted in 2007	Sets the enhanced use of renewable energy sources as a national priority
Law on Electricity and Natural Gas	National/ sectoral	Adopted in 1999, amended in 2013	Supports priority use of local hydro, and other renewable, alternative and gas resources
State Programme "Renewable Energy 2008"	National/ sectoral	Adopted in 2008, amended in 2013	Specifies rules and procedures for development of new renewable energy sources
Low Emission Development Strategy (LEDS)	National	Draft finalised as of August 2017	Identifies sectoral strategies and goals to achieve low-carbon development pathways
National Energy Efficiency Action Plan (NEEAP)	National	Finalised, and seeking government approval as of June 2017	Identifies energy emission targets, policy measures and financial needs
Nationally Appropriate Mitigation Actions (NAMAs)	Sectoral	Finalised	Developed NAMAs on biomass energy, buildings, sustainable forest management, transport and hydropower
National Forestry Concept for Georgia	Sectoral	Approved in 2013	Serves as a basis for sustainable development of the forest management and related policy frameworks
Sustainable Energy Action Plans (SEAPs) under the Covenant of Mayors	Municipal	10 SEAPs have been approved and submitted as of 2017	Shows the individual signatory municipalities' commitments to voluntarily reducing GHG emissions
Tbilisi Sustainable Urban Transport Strategy	Municipal/ sectoral	Finalised in 2016	Defines policy directions and priorities on sustainable transport to be implemented between 2015 and 2030
Green Economy Strategy	National/ sectoral	Under development	This will develop green economy interventions in various sectors, which can also lead to higher income and employment
Green City Action Plan of Tbilisi	Municipal	Under development	This will present benchmarking and priorities for tasks and defines the long-term Green City vision – within a timeframe of 10-15 years – supported by EBRBD
National Adaptation Plan (NAP)	National	Under development	This first draft will focus on the agriculture sector (being finalised as of October 2017)
National Renewable Energy Action Plan	National	Under development	This will develop a national policy framework for renewable energy sources, which is also compatible with Renewable Energy Directive 2009/28/EC
Climate Action Plan	National	Under development	This plan is being developed by the Ministry of Environment and Natural Resources Protection as an NDC implementation strategy

Source: Author's analysis based on Giely (2015), GoG (2016, 2015b, 2014, 2013a, 2013b, 2013c, 2007), MoESD (2017) and UNFCCC (2017).

The NDC describes Georgia's national targets on climate change mitigation and adaptation by 2030. The NDC does not include information on detailed actions to be taken, or robust examination of financial needs, to achieve the targets. Instead, the NDC refers to other official policy documents on climate mitigation actions, namely the Low Emission Development Strategy (LEDS) and the National Energy Efficiency Action Plan (NEEAP).

Georgia finalised LEDS in the middle of 2017 under the Enhancing Capacity for Low Emission Development Strategies Program with support of the United States Agency for International Development (USAID, 2017). LEDS aims to support Georgia's transition to a low-emission economy through various approaches. This will be achieved through the following, among others:

- identifying main sources of GHG emissions and their future trajectories
- setting goals and needed policy measures to tackle barriers to reducing GHG emissions in the selected sectors
- outlining necessary legislation systems, infrastructure and co-ordination for implementation
- proposing mechanisms to mobilise the national and international financial sources for implementation of LEDS (Winrock and Remmisia, 2017).

The government finalised the NEEAP in early 2017, seeking the government's approval as of August 2017. NEEAP documents detailed plans for horizontal energy-efficiency measures, such as financing scheme, energy auditing and performance labelling, as well as sector-specific measures. The latter includes measures on buildings, public bodies, industry, transport, heating and cooling, and energy transformation, transmission, distribution and demand response (NEEAP Expert Team, 2017). The following sub-sections discuss LEDS and NEEAP, as well as their potential roles in mobilising finance to achieve Georgia's climate targets.

Georgia has also been developing multiple nationally appropriate mitigation actions (NAMAs). These are also meant to be linked with the NEEAP (Mdivani and Hoppe, 2016). Georgian NAMAs focus on:

- adaptive sustainable forest management in Borjomi-Bakuriani Forest District (at the implementation stage)
- energy-efficient refurbishment in the public building sector (under development)
- efficient use of biomass for equitable, climate proof and sustainable rural development (under development)
- clean energy production in the Kakheti region (under development)
- urban transport sector (feasibility study) (UNFCCC, 2017).

The Technology Needs Assessment for Climate Change Mitigation, finalised in 2012, also identifies efficiency measures, as well as the stimulation of a range of renewable energy sources (e.g. wind, biomass, solar and geothermal) (GoG, 2012). The NDC also mentions the National Forestry Concept for Georgia, which serves as a basis for development of the sustainable forest management and related policy frameworks. The government also plans to develop more policy documents, such as a Green Economy Strategy and a national-level renewable energy action plan.

Several Georgian municipal governments have also developed and submitted their Sustainable Energy Action Plans (SEAPs) under the European Union's Covenant of Mayors initiative. It is notable that 18 self-governing cities and municipalities in Georgia have signed the Covenant of Mayors initiative, of which 11 have submitted SEAPs to voluntarily reduce their own GHG emissions. These SEAPs are expected to significantly contribute to implementation of Georgian climate mitigation actions (Covenant of Mayors, 2017; Remissia, 2017).

In addition to those documents discussed above, the government has developed and adopted various legal frameworks for renewable energy, especially hydropower. The Main Directions of the State Policy in Energy Sector of Georgia set the use of renewable energy sources as a national priority. It stresses relevant legal frameworks, scientific research, necessary infrastructure, and finance from domestic and foreign sources. The Law on Electricity and Natural Gas also highlights the importance of exploiting hydropower and other types of renewable energy in the country. For its part, the State Programme "Renewable Energy 2008" sets out rules and procedures for new renewable energy sources, as well as the basis for fixed electricity prices under guaranteed power purchase agreements (PPAs). The rules regarding the fixed electricity prices for hydropower and other renewable energy are under revision as of September 2017.

The Ministry of Energy is working with the United Nations Development Programme (UNDP) to develop a National Renewable Energy Action Plan (Ministry of Energy, 2017). Such a plan is needed partly because legal frameworks on renewable energy in Georgia do not fully comply with the Renewable Energy Directive 2009/28/EC in the light of the EU-Georgia Association Agreement and the Energy Community Treaty (Energy Community Secretariat, 2017).

Box 3.1. Financing climate action at the municipal level

Municipalities (including large cities such as Tbilisi and Batumi) face severe financial constraints to improve environmental quality and efficiency of their public infrastructure such as transport and buildings. The municipal budgets are generally too tight to meet all their investment needs for infrastructure and public services. As a result, infrastructure investment generally requires allocation of the central government budget and development finance from multilateral or bilateral sources. For instance, the Tbilisi Transport Company's income from subsidies (provided by the municipal government) and fares (paid by users) is not large enough to cover operational costs of public transport systems (Giely, 2015). The creditworthiness and borrowing capacity of municipalities, as well as the existing legal framework, are limited. They do not usually allow direct access to international development finance without approval of the Ministry of Finance (Singh, et al., 2016). It also remains unclear whether Georgian municipalities are sufficiently creditworthy to issue municipal bonds to finance infrastructure investment, including climate-related projects.

The high level of subsidies to urban transport makes sure that fares for public transport, such as metro and buses, are affordable for citizens. However, such subsidies have also strained the fiscal space of the municipal and central governments for investment in cleaner (i.e. lower GHG and air-pollutant emissions) and safer transport infrastructure. The city of Tbilisi allocates approximately half of its budget for public transport to finance the Tbilisi Transport Company (operator of public bus, metro and ropeway system in the city).

Municipalities recognise the importance of transport subsidies reform in the future. However, they also consider that other low cost, yet effective, policy measures should be taken first to ensure the acceptability of such reform. The city of Tbilisi has started developing the sustainable public transport system. For example, its Sustainable Urban Transport Investment Program has received the support of the Asian Development Bank (ADB), and it developed the Tbilisi Sustainable Urban Transport Strategy. Further, Tbilisi City Hall works on bus network restructuring with the support of the ADB, and bus fleet renewal with the loan from EBRD under its Green Cities Framework. The city of Batumi also seeks financial support of the EBRD under this framework, seeking a loan to finance electric and Euro 5 diesel-fuelled buses as of 2017.

> **Box 3.1. Financing climate action at the municipal level** *(continued)*
>
> In addition, the Municipal Project Support Facility (MPSF) was established in March 2015. It is available to support investment projects in municipalities of Georgia and other Eastern European and the Caucasus countries. The support is tailored to projects that address objectives of Sustainable Energy Action Plans (SEAPs) under the Covenant of Mayors initiative. The MPSF, funded through the EU's Neighbourhood Investment Facility (NIF), is managed by the European Investment Bank. Eligible project types include energy efficiency for public buildings, urban transport, district heating, renewable energy sources, solid waste management, and water supply and sanitation. Consulting services are also available for municipalities under the MPSF (European Commission, 2014).

Need for coherence among policy documents and strong stakeholder engagement

Table 3.3 outlines the NDC, LEDS, NEEAP and the Green Economy Strategy. They were developed relatively recently or remain under development, and have slightly different objectives and scopes. Notably, LEDS and NEEAP contain details on policy and

Table 3.3. **Sector coverage and objectives of national-level strategic documents on green growth and climate action in Georgia**

	NDC	LEDS	NEEAP	Green Economy Strategy
Energy supply	●	●	●	
Buildings	(●)*	●	●	
Transport	(●)*	●	●	(●)**
Industry (Energy use)	●	●	●	(●)**
Industrial processes	●	●		
Agriculture	●	●		(●)**
Waste	●	●		
LULUCF	(Annexed)	●		
Tourism	(●)*			(●)**
Construction	(●)*			(●)**
Investment needs	(● Only adaptation)	●	●	?
Mention of funding options		●	●	?
Objective	GHG emission reduction in general (adaptation also included)	GHG emission reduction in general	Energy efficiency	Improving economic competitiveness, while reducing resource use
Co-ordination role	MoENRP	MoENRP	MoE	MoESD
Status as of August 2017	Adopted	Document finalised	Document finalised	Under development

LULUCF: land use, land use change and forestry; **MoE**: Ministry of Energy; **MoENRP**: Ministry of Environment and Natural Resources Protection; **MoESD**: Ministry of Economy and Sustainable Development.

* These sectors are not explicitly mentioned in the NDC, but considered to be included according to Georgia's GHG Inventory and LEDS.

** Still under consideration as of June 2017.

Source: Author's analysis based on GoG (2015b), MoESD (2017), NEEAP Expert Team (2017), and Winrock and Remmisia (2017).

implementation (including on finance) to achieve the targets set under each document. As of September 2017, both LEDS and NEEAP have been finalised and are under government review.

The NDC and LEDS focus directly on mitigation of GHG emissions at the national level. NEEAP provides detailed targets on energy efficiency, planned measures and their expected results in the covered sectors. The Green Economy Strategy will examine economic competitiveness and inclusiveness (e.g. employment) in addition to resource efficiency in the sectors examined. Through development of the strategy, the government of Georgia has decided to establish an inter-ministerial working group on its green economy.

Georgia is still likely to need specific legal and/or policy frameworks to implement LEDS and NEEAP. Nevertheless, it has a clearer pathway to achieve its climate mitigation targets than when the INDC was submitted in 2015, and has planned policy measures at the national and sub-national levels. For instance, NEEAP outlines policy options such as energy efficiency in public buildings, energy audits, energy labelling, public procurement of energy-efficient goods and services, and awareness-raising. LEDS also outlines a range of policy instruments and needed investment projects for energy generation and distribution, energy use in buildings, transport and industrial facilities, non-energy related GHG emissions, and land use, land-use change and forestry (LULUCF), among others. Both LEDS and NEEAP are expected to inform development of regulations that will give actors incentives to cut energy use and GHG emissions in the country.

Ensuring coherence among these strategic policy documents will be crucial. Georgian stakeholders, in both public and private sectors, need to direct their financial resources to activities that contribute to low-carbon and inclusive growth. There is already some built-in coherence such as the use of the MARKAL Georgia Model for LEDS and NEEAP. Nevertheless, Table 3.3 illustrates overlaps in sectoral coverages between these policy documents. These imply a risk of lack, or an insufficient level, of coherence among these key strategy documents. This, in turn, could lead to issues in implementation such as inefficiency, unexpected obstacles and confusion among stakeholders.

Another important next step is to examine how these policies would help Georgia develop actual projects that will be needed to achieve its climate targets. Management of this process is likely to influence whether and how investors and businesses will fund climate-related projects. It is therefore timely to examine the following:

- how investors and businesses perceive development of these policies
- how these strategic documents can send stronger signals to investors
- what kind of implementation policies and engagement processes with the business sector of various sizes would be needed to enhance financial attractiveness of climate- and environment-related projects.

A well-designed communication strategy and stakeholder consultations are likely to help investors, industries, households and the public sector at various levels to understand these policy documents, targets and options for climate action. Such communication and engagement will be crucial for Georgia. They can ensure that strategic documents strengthen investor confidence and help tackle the information gap (See also Chapter 4.3). The information in LEDS and NEEAP can help further develop a list of climate-related projects that can be designed, financed and/or constructed in Georgia, especially for energy efficiency and non-hydro renewable energy. It can also help reduce non-energy related GHG emissions.

The contents of LEDS and NEEAP imply the importance of both measures to create demand for climate-related projects and activities, and funding mechanisms to meet the demand. LEDS and NEEAP both have dedicated sections on financing. These should be complemented and enhanced by a broader policy framework in Georgia, such as on investment promotion and facilitation, and financial market development (OECD, 2015; OECD-IEA-ITF-NEA, 2015).

For instance, NEEAP proposes a dedicated agency for promoting investment in infrastructure, goods and services related to energy efficiency (and potentially renewable energy) (NEEAP Expert Team, 2017). This agency could be extra-budgetary and have a longer budgeting period than one year (e.g. two to three years) to allow for flexible financial support to energy efficiency. The agency is not meant to be a financial institution. Instead, it delivers grant finance to catalyse public and private sector investment in energy efficiency, and donor co-ordination functions, among others. The agency could be capitalised by the government budget allocation first, but other channels could eventually contribute. These could include the allocation from energy bills, increased excise tax on energy-inefficient vehicles, and/or levy related to energy usage of corporations that failed to meet their energy-efficiency targets set in the context of NEEAP (NEEAP Expert Team, 2017).

The finance section of LEDS proposes multiple options to mobilising financing for climate action in Georgia, such as developing a climate finance strategy roadmap and establishing a national green investment bank. LEDS also proposes an inter-ministerial body called a Climate Finance Intelligence Task Force. This would centrally collect and manage information to support the government with planning, budgeting, policy analysis and design, market intelligence and other services. LEDS also emphasises better use of blended finance and exploring bond finance for climate-related projects and activities (Winrock and Remmisia, 2017).

NEEAP and LEDS both suggest options to scale up finance. These should be accompanied with enhanced engagement of the Ministry of Finance and private-sector entities (in both financial and non-financial sectors), as well as civil society organisations, over time. Private-sector actors have been involved in development of LEDS and NEEAP. However, there seems to be room for improved engagement of businesses at even earlier stages of policy development on climate and green growth agendas. Future revisions of the NDC, as well as development of the Green Economy Strategy, can benefit from more private-sector engagement. This will help various government ministries to further mainstream green issues into economic development policies and individual business practices. It can also enhance coherence among different policies, and address limited perception of climate- and green-related issues among the business sectors in the country.

Enhancing environmental regulations to drive investment demand for climate action

Georgian enterprises, from small- to large-sized ones, consider stricter environmental policies to be the most important lever for them to invest in energy efficiency and cleaner production, among other measures (Chorgolashvili, 2017). A survey under a United Nations Industrial Development Organization (UNIDO) project shows important factors that drive finance for resource efficiency and cleaner production by enterprises of various sizes. These include introduction of stricter regulations for energy efficiency and environmental protection. In addition, increased penalties for non-compliance rather than encouragement or additional benefits, are important factors (Figure 3.2). In addition to the survey results, some businesses indeed suggest that complying with stricter environmental regulation may create opportunities for them.

Figure 3.2. **Expected changes to regulations that would drive demand for resource-efficient and cleaner production**

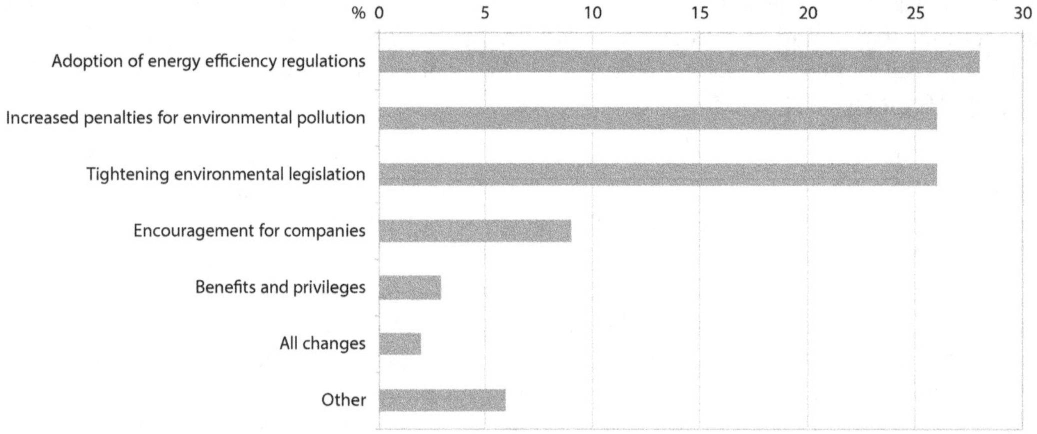

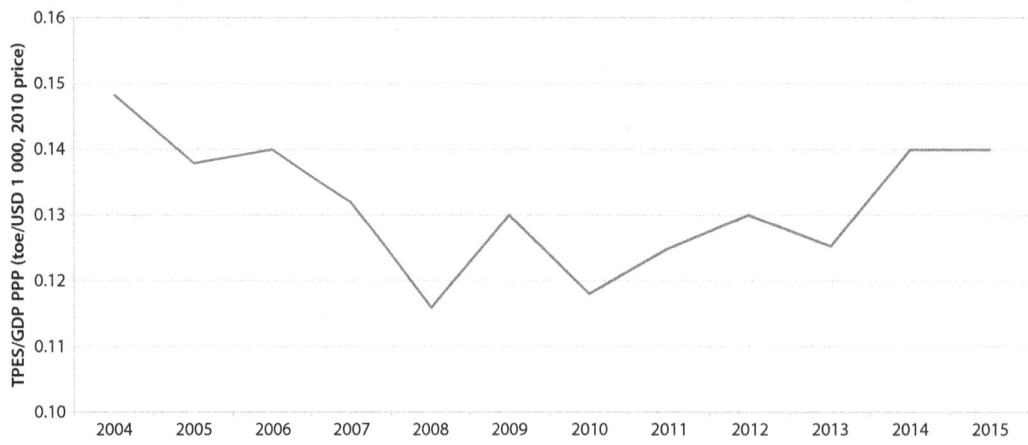

Note: Result from a survey research about opportunities and barriers to promote resource-efficient and cleaner production financing in Georgia under UNIDO.

Source: Chorgolashvili (2017).

While the government of Georgia has adopted laws and policy, the energy price is still too low to incentivise energy-efficiency finance. Further, environmental regulations remain relatively lenient. As a result, energy intensity has not markedly improved over the past decade, and has even increased in recent years (Figure 3.3.). As of June 2017, Georgia is the only country in the Eastern Europe, the Caucasus and Central Asia region, except Turkmenistan, that does not have any quantitative target for renewable energy or energy efficiency. However, LEDS and NEEAP can, and should, pave the way to enforceable policy measures to achieve targets under these documents. The Ministry of Energy and UNDP are also starting to develop a national-level renewable energy action plan.

Figure 3.3. **Trends in energy intensity in Georgia**

TPES: total primary energy supply; **toe**: tonnes oil equivalent; **PPP**: purchasing power parity.

Source: IEA (2017) World Energy Statistics (database), https://www.iea.org/statistics/.

NEEAP and potential subsequent legal frameworks to operationalise it are crucial to incentivise businesses and households to invest in energy efficiency. Various policy adopted over the past two decades has already mentioned the need for energy-efficiency measures. These include Presidential Decree No. 437 on Restructuring of the Power Sector, the Law on Electricity and Natural Gas, the Main Directions of State Policy in the Energy Sector and the Social-Economic Development Strategy of Georgia 2020.

Georgia has been one of the Energy Community Contracting Parties since July 2017 (Energy Community Secretariat, 2017). Being a Contracting Party should be a strong driver for, among others, renewable energy and energy-efficiency investments in Georgia to comply with several relevant EU Directives over time, such as Directive 2012/27/EU on energy efficiency. It also needs to implement Directive 2010/30/EU on labelling and standard product information on the consumption of energy and other resources (due on 31 December 2018). Directive 2010/31/EU on the energy performance of buildings should also be implemented by 30 June 2019. NEEAP already highlights these measures.

Further, several studies and policy documents, including NEEP, have pointed out the need for mandatory energy auditing across Georgian industry. Its implementation, however, will need to tackle the lack of local skills and expertise in industrial and building energy auditing (GoG, 2016). The draft Spatial Planning and Construction Code also incorporates energy-efficiency requirements for construction of new buildings (Energy Community Secretariat, 2017).

Table 3.4. **Summary of national-level mitigation policies in Georgia and benchmark countries**

	GEO	ALB	ARM	AZE	BLR	BIH	MKD	MDA	SRB	UKR
Regulatory policies for renewable energies										
Renewable energy targets		x	x	x	x	x	x	x	x	x
Biofuels obligation/mandate		x			x	x				
Electric utility quotas obligation/Renewable Portfolio Standard		x			x					
Feed-in tariff/premium payments	x	x	x	x	x	x	x	x	x	x
Heat obligation/mandate										
Net metering	x		x		x					x
Tendering (i.e. public bidding) for renewable energy	x	x				x				
Tradable renewable energies certificates		x			x					
Fiscal incentives for renewable energies and public financing										
Capital subsidy/rebate							x			
Energy production payment	x	x	x	x	x					x
Investment or production tax credits										x
Public investment, loans or grants	x		x	x				x	x	
Reduction in sales, energy, CO$_2$, VAT or other taxes								x		x
Energy-efficiency policies										
Energy-efficiency target		x			x	x	x	x	x	x
National energy-efficiency awareness campaigns	x			x	x	x	x	x	x	
National energy-efficiency regulations, standards or laws		x	x	x	x	x	x	x	x	x
Public institution(s) on energy-efficiency strategies and policies	x	x	x	x	x	x	x	x	x	x
Energy-efficiency labelling policies					x			x	x	x

ALB: Albania, **ARM**: Armenia, **AZE**: Azerbaijan, **BLR**: Belarus, **BIH**: Bosnia and Herzegovina, **MKD**: Former Yugoslav Republic of Macedonia, **MDA**: Moldova, **SRB**: Serbia and **UKR**: Ukraine.

Source: Based on UNECE and REN21 (2017).

Table 3.4. illustrates that Georgia has already put in place several climate-related policies. However, it is not necessarily a frontrunner in the field of energy efficiency or renewable energy. Other countries in Eastern Europe and Caucasus or in Central European countries with similar levels of GDP per capita (purchasing power parity, PPP) often have stronger policies especially for energy efficiency.

The transport sector has the largest share of energy-related GHG emissions in Georgia. However, Georgia has no effective environmental regulatory measures on road vehicles. This has at least partly contributed to the increase in outdated second-hand vehicles (often without catalytic converters). This, in turn, has led to a substantially high level of both air pollution in major Georgian cities and GHG emissions from road transport. Parking fees are also free or very low in cities, including Tbilisi. This also encourages the use of cars rather than public transport.

Need for energy subsidies reform

Relatively low energy prices in Georgia greatly help its populations access affordable energy. However, they keep energy-efficiency measures and smaller-scale renewable projects (e.g. decentralised solar power) economically unattractive. This low level of energy price is due to the low cost of domestic electricity generation, especially from hydropower. A subsidy for natural gas used for supplying electricity and heat is also a factor. (IEA, 2015; Singh, et al., 2016; Pavlenishivili, 2017; OECD, forthcoming) For instance, the government-regulated tariff for electricity from Enguri and Vardinili hydropower plants together generates more than 20% of electricity for Georgian territory. This is lower than 0.1 US cents per kWh (Zachmann, 2015). The balancing price of electricity in Georgia is around 5 US cents per kWh (Galt & Taggart, 2016).

The market prices of fuels such as natural gas and firewood do not reflect their production costs and are well below the prices for EU industries (GoG, 2016; Singh et al., 2016). Yet energy subsidies in Georgia aim to protect socially vulnerable groups from the impact of increases in electricity and natural gas tariffs (henceforth called "social gas"). Its level is relatively low compared to other Eastern European and the Caucasus countries (OECD, forthcoming). The size of subsidies to imported natural gas for energy generation and heat distribution is estimated at USD 228 million, or 1.4% of Georgia's GDP in 2014 (OECD, forthcoming). These subsidises take the form of providing gas at below market price and VAT exemptions.

As many other countries, reforms of energy subsidies have been socially and politically sensitive in Georgia. The Georgian government has taken steps to increase tax rates on certain fossil fuels. For instance, recent amendments to the Tax Code in January 2017 have caused an increase in the excise tax on fuel and motor oil for vehicles. Development of NEEAP has considered, but eventually not explicitly included, the energy subsidy reform as a priority measure for energy efficiency.

Energy costs that do not reflect prices on carbon emissions presumably have contributed to more natural gas and coal use in the country's total primary energy supply over the past few years (see Figure 3.4.). However, there seems to be a long list of hydropower projects to be constructed in the coming years. There has been a process of intensive gasification of some regions over the past years. This has improved affordable energy access, given that many households used to use biomass for heating and cooking (GoG, 2016). This shift has resulted from Georgia's effort to explore all avenues for diversifying energy supply to meet increasing demand and complement the seasonal fluctuation of hydropower generation

(IEA, 2015). At the same time, gasification also increased GHG emissions. It likely became an impediment to develop local renewable energy sources, such as decentralised solar panels (GoG, 2012; IEA, 2017).

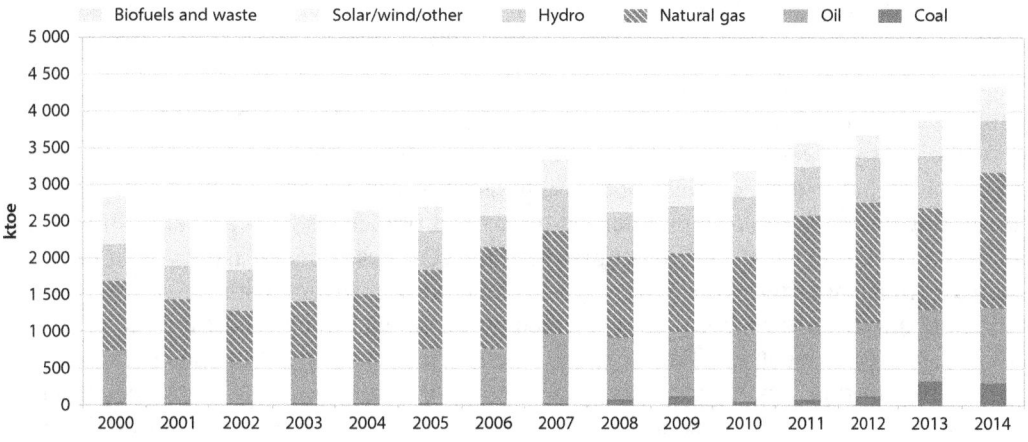

Figure 3.4. **Total primary energy supply by fuel (2000-14)**

Source: IEA (2017), World Energy Balances of non-OECD Countries 2015.

An increasing number of states have overcome the political obstacles to subsidy reforms, including developing countries such as India, Indonesia and Peru (OECD, 2017). Successful reforms generally have several features, including data on the monetary value of subsidies, their distribution across beneficiaries, and how energy-related services, air quality and/or GHG emissions could be improved when prices better reflect costs (OECD, 2017). An energy subsidy inventory in Georgia and other Eastern European and the Caucasus countries, developed by the OECD (forthcoming), can help Georgia pursue further reforms to energy subsidies by providing data on the monetary value of various energy subsidies.

It would also be useful to analyse the ability of Georgia's regulatory environment in encouraging competition and firm entry in light of improving both environmental policies and catalysing private-sector investments. A recent empirical analysis focusing on OECD and G20 countries shows that if regulatory restrictiveness is low, increased energy prices have a positive effect on investment (OECD, 2017; Prag and Röttgers, 2017). This means that firms will adapt to higher prices by increasing investment. Subject to data availability, this analysis could be done in Georgia in parallel with analyses of the supply side of green finance.

Greening public procurement

Public procurement rules can potentially contribute to creating significant demand by public bodies for low-carbon, climate-resilient goods and services. This, in turn, creates demand for finance to purchase them. The ratio of the government's expenditures for purchases of goods and services to GDP accounts for 18.4% in Georgia (World Bank, 2017). The government's allocation of this money can have a considerable impact on dissemination of products and services, including those that can facilitate climate action in the country (Baron, 2016).

Public procurement regulations and procedures in Georgia have evaluated tenders mostly based on their cost. However, the energy efficiency performance has not been adequately considered as of July 2017 (OECD, 2016b; Singh, et al., 2016). Georgia's regulations on public procurement commendably ensure competitive public tendering that aligns with EU practices. However, there is still room to improve use of public procurement to promote goods and services that can enhance environmental quality and social welfare. Georgia's State Procurement Agency could and should play an important role in integrating environmental or climate-related requirements into public procurement criteria.

There are already planned actions under NEEAP (NEEAP Expert Team, 2017). The public procurement scheme on energy efficiency proposed under NEEAP would be at both national and sub-national levels, for example. It would aim to reduce long-term operation and maintenance costs of the state and sub-national governments' property by decreasing energy bills for any procured goods and properties. It would also aim to help develop markets for energy-efficient products and services. This measure would integrate energy-efficiency criteria into public procurement in accordance with the law adopted in 2015, and develop a "rule book" for the green procurement scheme (NEEAP Expert Team, 2017). Large cities, such as Tbilisi, can also include technical specifications in their tender documents. In this way, they can promote energy-efficient goods and services, such as heating, ventilation and air conditioning, lighting and office equipment, through public procurement (Copenhagen Centre on Energy Efficiency, 2017).

Several initiatives across the world have used public procurement to disseminate goods and services with high-environmental performance (Table 3.5). Based on these experiences, as well as the OECD Recommendation of the Council on Public Procurement, Georgia should consider some caveats when designing green procurement schemes:

- Balance achievement of environmental/climate objectives and the primary procurement objectives.

- Build a capacity development component into the green procurement scheme to enable the workforce to support environmental/climate objectives.

- Monitor the benefits and costs of using procurement to achieve the environmental/climate objectives and periodically review them to inform policy-making

- Minimise the risk of an overload of objectives (Baron, 2016).

Table 3.5. **Examples of cross-boundary green public procurement initiatives**

Name of initiative	Description	Link
GPP 2020 consortium (Procurement for a Low-carbon Economy)	GPP 2020 brings together local and central government practitioners from some European countries. The consortium provides examples of low-carbon procurement projects and best practices, as well as open tenders.	www.gpp2020.eu/low-carbon-tenders/
Sustainable Procurement Platform (SPP)	ICLEI (Local Governments for Sustainability) established and manages SPP to share information, case studies, events, guidance, etc. on sustainable procurement from across the world.	www.sustainableprocurement.org/
The Global Sustainable Consumption and Production (SCP) Clearinghouse	The Clearinghouse consolidates knowledge on sustainable consumption and production from diverse regions and sectors.	www.scpclearinghouse.org/

Source: Based on GPP2020 (n.d.), ICLEI (n.d.) and UNEP (n.d.).

The level playing field between different renewable energy options

Preferential policy measures for hydropower and its untapped potential have successfully enhanced the hydropower project pipeline development in Georgia. This is generally a good thing. But they also seem to make it more challenging to draw private sector investors' attention to "non-hydro" renewable energy projects. Levelised costs[1] of wind and solar energy are still higher than most hydropower-generated electricity and other fossil fuel thermal power plants. They are also above regulated tariffs for the electricity system (e.g. Kühne et al., 2015; Pavlenishvili and Pignatti, 2016).

Some Georgian businesses have asked for a level playing field between hydropower and wind or solar energy. They claim that differentiated tariff policies and a long-term strategy for non-hydro renewable energy projects are necessary (GIG, 2017). For instance, the government and International Monetary Fund agreed to set fixed tariffs for renewables at no more than 6 US cents per kWh for eight months a year. This may be profitable for hydropower, but insufficient to make other types of renewable energy projects financially viable in Georgia.

Attractive short-term lending opportunities, such as retail banking (rather than corporate banking) often exacerbate a shortage of long-term capital that could be mobilised to finance climate action in Georgia. These opportunities are certainly positive for economic growth. However, they may make it more challenging to increase profiles of long-term investment in corporate banking and "non-hydro" renewable energy. Investment decision makers at financial institutions, as well as consumers and project developers, tend to favour investments in well-known technologies due to inexperience with alternatives. In addition, financial costs (including interest rates) tend to be higher for green projects, such as energy-efficiency projects, than for traditional mortgage loans. This makes these green projects less attractive for financial institutions and borrowers.

Note

1. Levelised cost of electricity (LCOE) is the net present value of the unit-cost of electricity over the lifetime of an electricity generating asset.

References

Baron, R. (2016), *The Role of Public Procurement in Low-carbon Innovation*, Background paper for the 33rd Round Table on Sustainable Development, 12-13 April 2016, OECD, Paris, https://www.oecd.org/sd-roundtable/papersandpublications/The%20Role%20of%20Public%20Procurement%20in%20Low-carbon%20Innovation.pdf.

Chorgolashvili, A. (2017), "Research about opportunities and barriers to promote RECP financing in Georgia", presentation to OECD workshop on green finance mobilisation in Georgia, Tbilisi, 23 June 2017. https://www.slideshare.net/OECD_ENV/session-6-presentation-by-unido (accessed 9 October 2017).

Copenhagen Centre on Energy Efficiency (2017), *Energy Efficiency Brief: Tbilisi, Georgia*, Copenhagen Centre on Energy Efficiency, http://kms.energyefficiencycentre.org/publication-report/energy-efficiency-brief-tbilisi-georgia.

Covenant of Mayors (2017), "Covenant of Mayors – Signatories", webpage, www.covenantofmayors.eu/about/about/signatories_en.html?commitments2=1&commitments3=1&commitments1=1 (accessed 9 June 2017).

Energy Community Secretariat (2017), *Energy Governance in Georgia, Report on Compliance with the Energy Community Acquis*, Energy Community Secretariat, Vienna, www.euneighbours.eu/sites/default/files/publications/2017-08/ECS_Georgia_Report_082017.pdf.

European Commission (2014), Municipal Project Support Facility (MPSF) – European Commission, Brussels, https://ec.europa.eu/europeaid/blending/municipal-project-support-facility-mpsf_en (accessed 9 October 2017).

Galt & Taggart (2016), *Georgia's Energy Sector Electricity Market Watch*, Galt & Taggart Research, Tbilisi.

Giely, J.-M. (2015), *Tbilisi Sustainable Urban Transport Strategy*, Sustainable Urban Transport Strategy, Municipal Development Fund of Georgia, Tbilisi.

GIG (2017), "Main obstacles for RES in Georgia", presentation by Georgian Industrial Group, presentation to OECD workshop on green finance mobilisation in Georgia, Tbilisi, 23 June 2017. https://www.slideshare.net/OECD_ENV/session-6-presentation-by-georgian-industrial-group (accessed 9 October 2017).

GoG (2016), *First Biennial Update Report on Climate Change*, Government of Georgia, Tbilisi, http://unfccc.int/files/national_reports/non-annex_i_parties/ica/application/pdf/first_bur_-_georgia.pdf.

GoG (2015a), *GHGs National Inventory Report of Georgia*, Government of Georgia, Tbilisi, http://unfccc.int/files/national_reports/non-annex_i_parties/biennial_update_reports/application/pdf/ghg_national_inventory_report___georgia.pdf.

GoG (2015b), *Georgia's Intended Nationally Determined Contribution*, Government of Georgia, Tbilisi, http://www4.unfccc.int/submissions/INDC/Published%20Documents/Georgia/1/INDC_of_Georgia.pdf.

GoG (2014), *Social-economic Development Strategy of Georgia: GEORGIA 2020*, Government of Georgia, Tbilisi, https://policy.asiapacificenergy.org/sites/default/files/Georgia%202020_ENG.pdf.

GoG (2013a), *Georgian Law on Electricity and Natural Gas*, Government of Georgia, Tbilisi, www.gnerc.org/uploads/kanoni.pdf.

GoG (2013b), *Decree #107 State Program "Renewable Energy 2008"*, Government of Georgia, Tbilisi, https://policy.asiapacificenergy.org/sites/default/files/State%20Program%20%E2%80%9CRenewable%20Energy%202008%E2%80%9D%20about%20Approval%20of%20the%20Rule%20to%20Enable%20the%20Construction%20of%20Renewable%20Energy%20Sourcesin%20Georgia.pdf.

GoG (2013c), *National Forest Concept for Georgia*, Government of Georgia, Tbilisi, http://w3.cenn.org/wssl/uploads/home/National%20forest%20policy%20for%20georgia%20(ENG).pdf.

GoG (2012), *Technology Needs Assessment and Technology Action Plans for Climate Change Mitigation*, Government of Georgia, Tbilisi, http://unfccc.int/ttclear/misc_/StaticFiles/gnwoerk_static/TNR_CRE/e9067c6e3b97459989b2196f12155ad5/e8e037dbb07b4a348c1f21ca63443cb7.pdf.

GoG (2007), *Main Direction of the State Policy in Energy Sector of Georgia*, Government of Georgia, Tbilisi, www.energy.gov.ge/projects/pdf/pages/MAIN%20DIRECTIONS%20OF%20THE%20STATE%20POLICY%20IN%20ENERGY%20SECTOR%20OF%20201047%20eng.pdf.

GPP2020 (n.d.), "Low-carbon Tenders", webpage, www.gpp2020.eu/low-carbon-tenders/ (accessed 8 September 2017).

ICLEI (n.d.), Sustainable Procurement Platform website, www.sustainable-procurement.org/ (accessed 8 September 2017).

IEA (2017), *World Energy Balances of non-OECD Countries 2015* (database), https://www.iea.org/statistics/statisticssearch/report/?country=Georgia&product=balances (accessed 28 August 2017).

IEA (2015), *Energy Policies Beyond IEA Countries: Caspian and Black Sea Regions 2015*, OECD Publishing, Paris, http://dx.doi.org/10.1787/9789264228719-en.

Kühne, M, et al. (2015), *Perspectives for Electricity Generation from Renewable Energy Sources in the South Caucasus Region*, CAUCASUS ANALYTICAL DIGEST No. 69, 26 January 2015, www.css.ethz.ch/content/dam/ethz/special-interest/gess/cis/center-for-securities-studies/pdfs/CAD-69-11-15.pdf.

Mdivani, K. and T. Hoppe (2016), "Experience with LEDS and NAMA Low Carbon Strategies: The case of Georgia", *Sustainability*, Vol. 8/6, MDPI, Basel, pp. 535, http://dx.doi.org/10.3390/su8060535.

Ministry of Energy (2017), *More Renewables and Improved Energy Efficiency: Energy Policy in Georgia*, Ministry of Energy of Georgia, Tbilisi, https://www.unece.org/fileadmin/DAM/env/documents/2017/WAT/04Apr_11_5SC/GE_5SC_Arabidze_EN.pdf.

MoESD (2017), *Green Economy Strategy Development*, Ministry of Economy and Sustainable Development, Tbilisi.

NEEAP Expert Team (2017), *Draft National Energy Efficiency Action Plan*, report commissioned by European Bank for Reconstruction and Development, London.

OECD (forthcoming), *Inventory of Energy Subsidies in the EU's Eastern Partnership Countries*, OECD Publishing, Paris.

OECD (2017), *Investing in Climate, Investing in Growth*, OECD Publishing, Paris, http://dx.doi.org/10.1787/9789264273528-en.

OECD (2016a), *Financing Climate Action in Georgia*, OECD Publishing, Paris, http://www1.oecd.org/environment/outreach/Georgia_Financing_Climate_Action.Nov2016.pdf.

OECD (2016b), *Promoting Better Environmental Performance of SMEs: Georgia*, www.oecd.org/env/outreach/Georgia%20pilot%20project%20report%20final%20EN.pdf.

OECD (2015), *Policy Guidance for Investment in Clean Energy Infrastructure: Expanding Access to Clean Energy for Green Growth and Development*, OECD Publishing, Paris, http://dx.doi.org/10.1787/9789264212664-en.

OECD-IEA-ITF-NEA (2015), *Aligning Policies for a Low-carbon Economy*, OECD Publishing, Paris, http://dx.doi.org/10.1787/9789264233294-en.

Paresishvili, G. (2017), *Georgian Stock Exchange: Georgian Capital Market Development*, https://www.saras.gov.ge/Content/files/GSE-Capital-Market-Development-FINAL-ENG-19.06.17.pdf.

Pavlenishvili, L. and N. Pignatti (2016), Net Metering in Georgia. Getting Ready for the Next Energy Revolution, www.iset-pi.ge/index.php/en/iset-economist-blog-2/entry/net-metering-in-georgia-getting-ready-for-the-next-energy-revolution.

Prag, A. and D. Röttgers (2017), *State-Owned Enterprises and the Low-Carbon Transition*, OECD Publishing, Paris.

Remissia (2017), "Sustainable Energy Action Plan", webpage, http://remissia.ge/eng-seap-page41.html (accessed 10 October 2017).

Singh, J. et al. (2016), *Energy Efficiency Financing Option Papers for Georgia*, World Bank, Washington, DC, http://documents.worldbank.org/curated/en/825761475845097689/Energy-efficiency-financing-option-papers-for-Georgia.

UN Environment (n.d.), SCP Clearinghouse website, www.scpclearinghouse.org/ (accessed 8 October 2017).

UNECE and REN21 (2017), *UNECE Renewable Energy Status Report 2017*, United Nations Economic Commission for Europe, Geneva,. https://www.unece.org/fileadmin/DAM/energy/se/pp/renew/Renewable_energy_report_2017_web.pdf.

UNFCCC (2017), *Georgia – NAMA* (database), www.nama-database.org/index.php/Georgia (accessed 9 May 2017).

USAID (2017), *Georgia Overview, EC-LEDS*, United States Agency for International Development, Washington, DC, https://www.ec-leds.org/countries/georgia.

Winrock and Remmisia (2017), "Georgia Low Emission Development Strategy Draft Report", commissioned by the USAID-funded EC-LEDS Clean Energy Program, Winrock International and Sustainable Development Center, Remissia, Tbilisi.

World Bank (2017), *World Development Indicators*, World Bank Group, http://wdi.worldbank.org/tables (accessed 31 October 2017).

Zachmann, G. (2015), "Can low electricity prices be a comparative advantage of Georgia?", *Policy Paper Series*, No. PP/02/2015, German Economic Team Georgia, Tbilisi, www.get-georgia.de/wp-content/uploads/2014/11/PP_02_2015_en.pdf.

Chapter 4

Channels of finance for climate action in Georgia

This chapter takes stock of existing financial channels available for a range of climate action in Georgia. These channels include the central and municipal governments, which invested directly in infrastructure and risk mitigation instruments. State-owned enterprises, sovereign equity funds, domestic commercial banks and other types of Georgian financial institutions have also provided finance. Bilateral and multilateral donors provide development finance as well. Finally, the chapter explores new financial channels for green finance that may be used for Georgia's climate action in future. Green bonds, for example, are attracting more interest.

Stocktaking of financial channels for climate-related investment

Taxpayers and users ultimately fund development of infrastructure. However, national and sub-national governments, public- and private-sector financial institutions, businesses and development financial institutions can often finance various phases of its development. Georgia has been successfully increasing private-sector investments in domestic fixed capital stock over the past few years (Figure 4.1). This is largely due to its effort on deregulation, streamlining tax systems, improved market transparency and promotional activities, among other factors. After the sharp decline in 2008 and 2009 due to the global financial crisis, investment in fixed capital stock in Georgia has constantly increased, reaching the record high level of USD 5.42 billion in 2015. More than 80% is provided by private sector investment.

Figure 4.1. **Investment in fixed capital stock in Georgia (2001-15)**

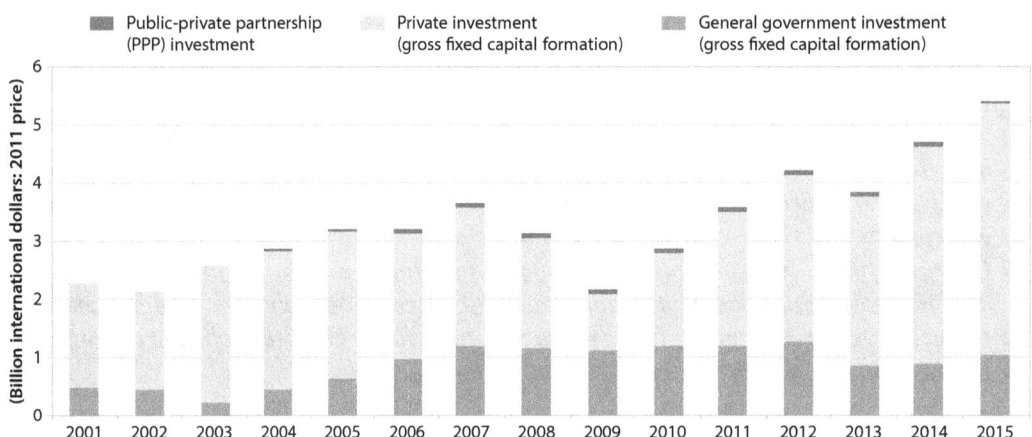

Source: Based on IMF (2017), Investment and Capital Stock Dataset 1960-2015 (January 2017 version).

Nevertheless, it remains unclear how much of the investment in the fixed capital stock in Figure 4.1 also targets climate change mitigation or adaptation. Typical characteristics of green finance include high up-front capital costs, long payback periods and greater reliance on regulatory frameworks (e.g. prices on carbon). These features often lead to a greater need for public-sector financing. This is implicitly reflected in the cost estimates under NEEAP as shown in Figure 2.2 in Chapter 2.2. It estimates that central and municipal governments, as well as state-owned entities, will finance more than 40% of investment in energy efficiency.

Mobilising further finance to achieve the long-term targets on Georgia's climate and green growth agendas will require a multi-faceted approach:

- scaling up of finance from already available channels especially in the private sector (e.g. commercial banks)
- better use of public sector finance from international and domestic sources (e.g. blended finance with a greater catalytic effect)
- exploration of new channels not yet commonly used for financing climate action, but with a certain potential in Georgia.

Table 4.1. Examples of financial channels already or potentially available for financing climate action in Georgia

		Domestic							International				
		Public			Private				Public			Private	
		Central government	Municipal government	Sovereign funds	Domestic commercial banks	Micro-finance institutions	Institutional investors	(Non-financial corporations)	Development banks	Bilateral donors	International climate funds	Financial institutions	(Non-financial corporations)
Debt	Sovereign bonds	1**	2	N/A	N/A	N/A	N/A	N/A	N/A	N/A	N/A	N/A	N/A
	Corporate bonds	N/A	N/A	N/A	2	2	2	2	1	N/A	N/A	2	2
	Project bonds	N/A	N/A	2	2	N/A	2	2	2	N/A	2	2	2
	Direct lending/co-investment lending	N/A	N/A	1	1	2	2	N/A	1	1	2	1	N/A
	Green credit-lines extended by IFIs	N/A	N/A	N/A	(Channel)	(Channel)	N/A	N/A	1	1	2	N/A	N/A
Mixed	Mezzanine financing	N/A	N/A	1	1	1	1	N/A	1	2	2	2	N/A
Equity	Direct investment	1	1	1	N/A	2	1	1	1	1	1	1	N/A
	Equity funds	N/A	N/A	N/A	N/A	N/A	N/A	N/A	2	1	2	1	N/A
Risk mitigation instruments	Grants	1	1	2	N/A	N/A	N/A	N/A	1	1	1	N/A	N/A
	Revenue guarantees*	1	N/A	N/A	N/A	N/A	N/A	N/A	N/A	N/A	N/A	N/A	N/A
	Technical assistance	1	1	N/A	N/A	N/A	N/A	N/A	1	1	1	N/A	N/A
	Interest rate subsidies	1	N/A	N/A	N/A	N/A	N/A	N/A	N/A	1	2	N/A	N/A
	Guarantees/insurance	2	N/A	1	N/A	N/A	N/A	N/A	1	1	2	2	N/A
	Fund seeding	2	2	2	2	2	N/A	N/A	1	1	1	2	N/A
	Currency swaps	N/A	N/A	N/A	N/A	N/A	N/A	N/A	2	2	2	1	N/A
	Securitisation	N/A	N/A	2	N/A	N/A	2	N/A	2	2	2	2	2
	Pooling/aggregation	N/A	N/A	2	N/A	N/A	2	N/A	2	2	2	2	2

1: Financial channels available; **2**: Channels potentially available, but not used yet; **N/A**: not applicable

* Revenue guarantees include power purchase agreements (PPAs) that may be eliminated in the near future.
** Georgia's budget code does not allow for earmarked budget for any purposes, including expenditure on climate-related projects.
Source: Author's analysis.

Table 4.1 summarises possible financial channels. It examines major capital sources that can provide finance for climate action in Georgia. Further, it illustrates financial instruments that are available, or can potentially be used in future, for climate action in the country. Sections 4.1.1 to 4.1.5 provide examples and narratives of these existing financial channels; section 4.2 looks at potentially available channels. Chapter 5 discusses the implication of various investment-related policies for mobilisation of financial instruments that might be used in the future.

Table 4.1 categorises capital sources into public and private, and international and domestic institutions. Financial instruments that can be used to deliver or catalyse green finance are also diverse. These include fixed income financing, such as loans and bonds; mezzanine (a hybrid of debt and equity financing) finance; and equity. Risk mitigation instruments and mechanisms can help mobilise finance for climate action. They include risk mitigants (e.g. guarantees, insurance, currency risk protection instruments, and public investments or grants) and transaction enablers (e.g. securitisation, pooling and aggregation). With respect to fixed assets and working capital at small- and medium-sized enterprises (SMEs), each company's internal resources (i.e. balance sheet investment) provide about 80% of finance (EIB, 2016).

To date, some of the financial channels and risk mitigation instruments in Table 4.1 have been regularly used only for hydropower projects. These include equity investment and most of the direct lending, as well as mezzanine finance by domestic sources and international private-sector financial institutions. Energy efficiency and other types of renewable energy have benefited much less, or not at all, from these financial channels. Exceptions include a small number of wind and solar power projects funded by a sovereign equity fund, the Georgian Energy Development Fund. Moreover, the government of Georgia is planning to reform its policies on power purchase agreements (PPAs) for hydropower and renewable energy. This will eliminate PPAs as a risk mitigation instrument.

Central and municipal governments

The central and municipal governments have invested directly in infrastructure and provided risk mitigation instruments. These include, for instance, fixed tariffs set under power purchase agreements (PPA) for hydropower and other types of renewable energy projects. Both types of government finance seem to constitute a substantial share of green finance in the country. Tbilisi City Hall also invests in energy efficiency in ten public-sector buildings in the city (Copenhagen Centre on Energy Efficiency, 2017).

In 2017, the central government plans to significantly raise public investment for capital expenditures with a focus on road, energy and seaport infrastructure. It plans to increase the ratio of gross public investment to gross domestic product (GDP) from 6.5% in 2016 to 8% in 2017 and 9% in 2020 (Tan and Dolidze, 2017). Nonetheless, it is still unclear how much of the public investment plans to be directed to climate-related projects.

Electricity-sector PPAs have been agreed between the government, the Electricity System Commercial Operator (ESCO) and the project sponsors. They have been a crucial risk mitigation instrument for the private sector and many development finance institutions for investment decisions in hydropower plants and other types of energy projects (e.g. Qartli Wind Farm project). The government's support for hydropower has multiple objectives: create jobs; reduce overall electricity costs; increase revenue from electricity export; strengthen energy independence; and avoid GHG emissions that would occur if thermal power plants were put in place instead.

The large volume of electricity guaranteed by the PPAs, however, can also pose substantial fiscal risks to the government and Georgian state-owned entities in the energy sector (World Bank, 2015). Upon the recommendation of the International Monetary Fund (IMF), the Ministry of Energy placed a moratorium on existing PPA policy in 2016. The moratorium was later suspended (Galt & Taggart, 2016). Subsequently, the government introduced the standard term and price for the mandatory sale of electricity. The ESCO now purchases the full volume of generated electricity during the eight winter months for up to 6 US cents per kWh. Nevertheless, the government of Georgia is revising the rules regarding tariffs for renewable energy as of October 2017. Under the new rules, the government would discuss terms for each project separately and agree on the individual tariff/price level.

The Georgian Ministry of Finance has issued sovereign bonds (treasury bonds) with various maturities to foster the domestic capital market, which was also driven by investor demand. The coupon has steadily fallen despite some fluctuations. Recently, it recorded the lowest rate (9.4% in 2017 for ten-year treasury bonds) since its first issuance in 2012. In theory, Georgia could issue a sovereign green bond (discussed in Chapter 4). However, the current Budget Code of Georgia does not allow allocation of any revenues for specific purposes, including climate-related activities in Georgia.

Sovereign funds

State-owned equity funds, namely JSC Georgian Energy Development Fund and JSC Partnership Fund, provide equity financing to hydropower plants and some emerging "non-hydro" renewable energy. For example, the Georgian Energy Development Fund, together with the Georgian Oil and Gas Corporation, are the shareholders of Qartli Wind Farm, the first wind power plant in the country, as of August 2017. The European Bank for Reconstruction and Development (EBRD) provides the project with a ten-year loan of USD 22.0 million. In principle, the Georgian Energy Development Fund is meant to be a minority shareholder of a joint venture for its project. Preferably, it holds less than 30% of equity, or 10% of total project investment costs, and has exit options for the project.

The investment in the Qartli Wind Farm may have an important demonstration effect. Specifically, it could attract a wider set of investors towards further development of wind power plants in Georgia. Moreover, the government announced plans for a public offering of the Qartli Wind Farm on the Georgian Stock Exchange in 2017. This move aims to encourage development of the stock exchange. It will also raise awareness among citizens regarding Georgia's wind power potential through opportunities to purchase shares of the wind firm (Agenda.GE, 2017). The Georgian Energy Development Fund also plans investments in further wind energy projects (Khaindrava, 2017).

Another sovereign equity fund, JSC Partnership Fund, has no "green" mandate, but is seeking opportunities for green investment. The Partnership Fund has invested in the facility that produces energy-efficient construction material (building blocks) of Ytong Caucasus (Partnership Fund, 2016). This investment followed Georgia's obligation, as part of the Association Agreement with the European Union (EU), to ensure energy-efficient construction. Georgia produces little energy-efficient construction material. As a result, the Partnership Fund invested in the factory that could supply energy-efficient construction blocks to the Georgian market. It could also sell markets in neighbouring countries such as Armenia, Azerbaijan and part of the Russian Federation. Further, the Partnership Fund also provides co-financing to hydropower projects in Georgia.

As another sign of possible increase in climate-related investments, the Partnership Fund is applying for accreditation with the Green Climate Fund (GCF). Becoming an accredited entity will enable the Partnership Fund to directly access the GCF's financial resources. This, in turn, will allow it to blend finance to scale up further investments in climate action in the country. The accreditation process is often lengthy. However, direct access to GCF is expected to considerably strengthen the ownership of Georgia in accessing, managing and allocating financial resource for climate action. It may also reduce transaction costs (Masullo et al., 2015).

Domestic commercial banks

Georgian commercial banks are a key provider of finance to infrastructure and building stocks. They also fund shorter-term assets such as production capital and machinery in Georgia. Commercial banks hold more than nearly 93% of total assets in the country (National Bank of Georgia, 2016). In recent years, the scale of commercial bank loans has kept increasing (Figure 4.2).

Figure 4.2. **Volume and growth rate of commercial bank loans in Georgia**

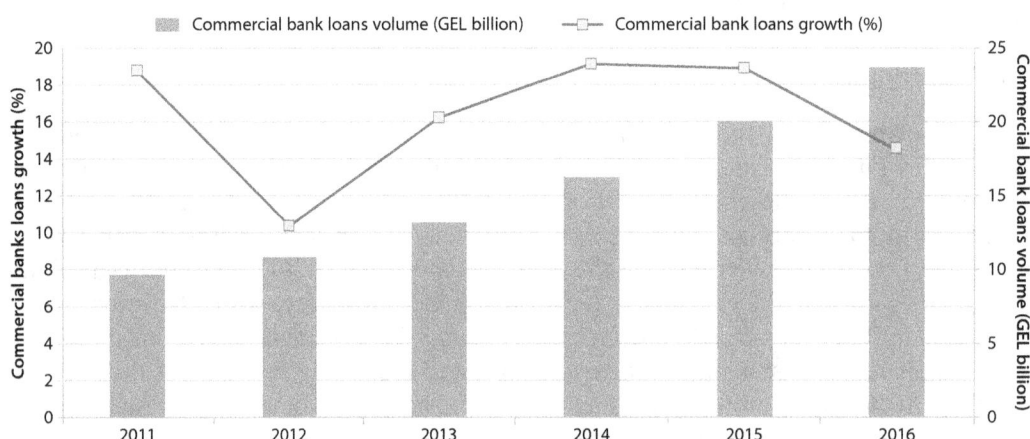

GEL: Georgian Laris (1 GEL= approximately USD 0.4 as of August 2017)

Source: Author's analysis based on National Bank of Georgia (2017).

In Georgia, some domestic commercial banks provide debt financing to certain types of renewable energy. These include large- and small-scale hydropower projects, as well as energy-efficiency measures to a lesser extent. For instance, JSC Bank of Georgia, a leading Georgian bank with a 31.5% of market share for loans in the country, has provided debts (loans) to construct several hydropower projects (Bank of Georgia, 2014). BGEO group, the parent company of JSC Bank of Georgia, owns a water utility company in Tblisi, Georgian Water and Power, with hydropower facilities. JSC ProCredit Bank Georgia also provides mainly small and medium sized enterprises with Green Loan products to energy efficiency and renewable energy, which accounts for around 12% of the bank's total loan portfolio (Box 4.1.). Georgian commercial banks also channel environmental credit lines extended by bilateral and multilateral development banks as discussed in 4.1.5.

> **Box 4.1. Greening the loan operation and management system of Procredit Bank Georgia**
>
> ProCredit Bank Georgia, as a part of the ProCredit group based in Germany, focuses mainly on financial services for small and medium-sized enterprises (SMEs) with long-term business plans. Fitch Ratings awarded ProCredit Bank Georgia with a rating of BB/Stable. This is the highest rating for any Georgian enterprise, and above the sovereign rating.
>
> The ProCredit group incorporates promotion of environmental awareness and protection, including climate change mitigation, into a critical part of its business model. Further, it does this both in its business operations and in the day-to-day work by staff. ProCredit Bank Georgia and the other banks of the ProCredit Group have a comprehensive, three-pillar environmental management system (EMS). It aims to improve both the internal and external environmental impact of the banks' activities. In 2016, ProCredit Bank Georgia completed the ISO 14001:2015 certification process.
>
> Environmental management and green finance fit with the ProCredit approach to building long-term client relationships. Commitment to environmental management and offering green financing is "a point of differentiation" for the Procredit Bank to acquire, retain and deepen relationships with its clients. It also connects directly to the overarching topic of operational efficiency and productivity, which is vital for SMEs, especially producers, in all markets.
>
> The Green Loan Portfolio accounts for around 12% of the ProCredit Bank Georgia's total loan portfolio. The bank offers three categories of green loans consisting of investments in energy efficiency, renewable energy and other areas that have positive impacts on the environment. The ProCredit group defines an energy-efficiency investment as one that improves a client's energy efficiency. This might include, for example, installation of more efficient equipment to achieve significant energy savings. Among other areas, ProCredit Bank Georgia invests in renewable energy technologies, primarily in solar water heaters; photovoltaic installations; small hydropower plants and wind power turbines; and biogas and biomass applications.
>
> ProCredit Bank Georgia only designs and provides new types of loans for green purposes. Further, it devotes resources to awareness-raising campaigns and regular training sessions for the bank's staff, enabling them to improve environmental performance of clients. The ProCredit Academy in Germany provides comprehensive training for staff members at both the bank level and the group level.
>
> To raise customer awareness, ProCredit Bank Georgia started its "Come and See" project. Clients are invited to share their successful experiences with each other, discussing how ProCredit Bank recommendations have helped them develop their business and achieve their business objectives.
>
> For further information, see ProCredit Bank Georgia (2017).

Other private sector investors

Private-sector investors that can finance climate-related projects in Georgia also include equity funds and (non-financial sector) corporations. However, finance from these investors remains smaller than loans from commercial banks in Georgia, and is mostly concentrated on hydropower. The country has rich hydropower resources, favourable regulations such as income guarantees through PPAs, exemptions from value-added tax (VAT), and relatively simple and transparent trade and investment regimes. These have helped make hydropower projects an "investment-grade" asset class. See also WTO (2015).

As shown in Table 4.2, both domestic and international investors and corporations finance renewable energy projects in Georgia. For instance, a Georgian equity fund, JSC Caucasus Energy & Infrastructure, focuses on greenfield investments in small and medium-sized hydropower plants in Georgia. The Georgian Co-Investment Fund, the largest private-sector equity fund in Georgia, also invests in three hydropower projects. These include acquisition of the 48 MW Mtkvari Small Hydro Power Plant from JSC Caucasus Energy & Infrastructure, whose construction will be completed in 2019 (Georgian Co-Investment Fund, 2014). A special purpose vehicle sponsored by Norway-based Clean Energy Investment Group, Indian Tata Power and the International Finance Corporation (IFC) also invests in 178 MW Shuakhevi HPP, 9 MW Skhalta HPP and 110 MW Koromkheti HPP.

Corporations, either Georgian companies or joint ventures with foreign capital, also invest in hydropower projects, especially using equity finance from their balance sheet. Georgian Industrial Group, the largest Georgian holding company, owns and operates thermal and hydropower plants with a total installed capacity of 662 MW (Gas TPPs:300 MW, HPPs49 MW and Coal TPPs 13 MW). The Georgian Water and Power Ltd, the largest Georgian water supply and sanitation service provider, has also invested in Zhinvali and Tetrikhevi HPPs. JSC Energo-Pro Georgia, a subsidiary of a Czech utility company, owns 15 hydropower plants. Turkish companies also invest in special purpose vehicles (SPVs) and joint ventures for hydropower projects such as Achar Energy 2007 Ltd., Calik Enerji and Georgia-Urban Energy LLC, which develop and operate several hydropower plants. Adjaristqali Georgia LLC is an SPV sponsored by Norway-based Clean Energy Investment Group, Tata Power and the IFC with the aim to invest in 178 MW Shuakhevi HPP, 9 MW Skhalta HPP and 110 MW Koromkheti HPP.

The Georgian Co-Investment Fund's deal to acquire the Mtkvari Small Hydro Power Plant also implies the potential to explore a secondary market for renewable energy infrastructure investment. This, in turn, could be boosted by mergers and acquisitions and refinancing activities. In theory, refinancing can lower overall financing costs for electricity generation, and potentially free up fiscal space for the government (OECD, 2015).

Table 4.2 also illustrates that climate-related finance by private sector investors has been largely concentrated on hydropower projects. Further, it shows private sector investment in wind and solar is still in its early days. In addition, equity financing is still a small fraction of financial instruments used in the country to date. However, increasing equity finance is a government priority in light of its capital market development. Mobilising the climate-related projects of such equity funds and (non-financial) corporations requires enhanced understanding of the appetites and needs of these actors for risk and liquidity in investments, and their capacity (OECD, 2017a). It also requires robust and stable climate policies and enabling environments for investment promotion as discussed in Chapter 3.

Lease financing, in which a leasing company allows a customer to use its equipment for a specified length of time (lease term), could mobilise finance for energy efficiency and renewable energy in general. However, it is little used in Georgia. The total volume of leasing transactions amounts to GEL 100 million (USD 40.4 million), with SME share slightly over 10% (EIB, 2016). Leasing generally does not require additional collateral. The high collateral required for bank loans is a major barrier to Georgian SMEs. Thus, leasing could greatly help them finance fixed assets, including energy efficiency and renewable energy-related equipment (see Chapter 5.1.1). Leasing also often offers more flexible repayment structures than general bank lending.

Table 4.2. **Examples of private-sector investors in renewable energy in Georgia (excluding commercial banks)**

Company name	Description
Achar Energy 2007 Ltd.	A subsidiary of Turkish Eksim Investment Holding A.Ş, investing in Chorokhi Downstream hydropower plant (HPP) projects
Adjaristqali Georgia LLC	Special purpose vehicle sponsored by Norway-based Clean Energy Investment Group, Tata Power and IFC with the aim to invest in 178 MW Shuakhevi HPP, 9 MW Skhalta HPP and 110 MW Koromkheti HPP
Calik Enerji	A Turkish holding company planning to build two wind power plants in Georgia with a total capacity of 170 MW (50 MW in Nigozi and 120 MW in Sachkhere)
Caucasus Energy & Infrastructure (CEI)	A private equity fund that concentrates on greenfield investments in small and medium-sized HPPs
Energo-Pro Georgia	Distribution network operator that owns and operates 15 small and medium-sized HPPs with a cumulative capacity of 469 MW; as well as one thermal power plant
Georgian Co-Investment Fund	A Georgian private equity fund with USD 6 billion of assets that invests in, among others, Tskhenistskali cascade HPPs, Oni cascade HPPs and Mktvari HPP
Georgian Industrial Group	The largest Georgian holding company that owns and operates thermal and hydropower plants with a total installed capacity of 662 MW (gas thermal power plants: 300 MW, HPPs 49MW and Coal TPPs 13MW)
Georgian Renewable Power Company	A subsidiary of BGEO Group, holding majority stake in Svaneti Hydro and Zoti Hydro, and participating in Mestiachala-1, Mestiachala-2 and Zoti HPPs
Georgian Water and Power Ltd.	Largest Georgian water supply and sanitation service provider, also Zhinvali and Tetrikhevi HPPs
Georgia-Urban Energy LLC.	A company, owned by a Turkish holding company Anadolu Grubu, which has the majority stake of 87 MW Paravani HPP
Hydrolea	A Georgian-Bulgarian company that owns and operates the 9 MW Akhmeta and 3 MW Debeda HPPs
Peri Ltd.	Georgian construction company that holds stakes in 19 MW Larsi HPP, 5 MW Khadori-2 HPP, 108 MW Dariali HPP and Oni cascade HPPs, among others
Transelectrica	A project company working on the 702 MW Khudoni HPP project, 34 km upstream the Enguri River from the Enguri Arch Dam.

Source: Author's analysis.

Box 4.2. JSC m2 Real Estate's investment in electric vehicle chargers

Under a social programme called "More Oxygen in City", JSC m2 Real Estate, a subsidiary of BGEO Group, invests in a project by E-Space LLC to install electric vehicle (EV) chargers throughout Georgia. The programme aims at enabling hybrid and electric cars to cover the distance from Telavi to Batumi on a single charge. The capital expenditure amounts to EUR 100 000. This will be covered by m2 Real Estate's corporate social responsibility programme, and used to install 20 charging stations for EVs. E-Space LLC plans to install up to 100 EV chargers at gas stations, hotels and supermarkets owned by partner organisations for the coming years. The charging stations can be used free of charge until the end of 2017, while fees will be applied to cover variable and maintenance costs from 2018.

Source: Caucasus Business Week (2016).

Development finance institutions

Table 4.1 also shows that international development finance institutions and bilateral donors continue to play a crucial role in mobilising green finance in Georgia. They help mobilise green finance both by providing financial resources and bringing knowledge, expertise and innovation based on broad experience in Georgia and elsewhere (OECD, 2017a, 2016). Development finance institutions include multilateral development banks, bilateral development banks and agencies, and international climate funds.

Figure 4.3. **Annual climate-related development finance committed to Georgia in 2013-15**

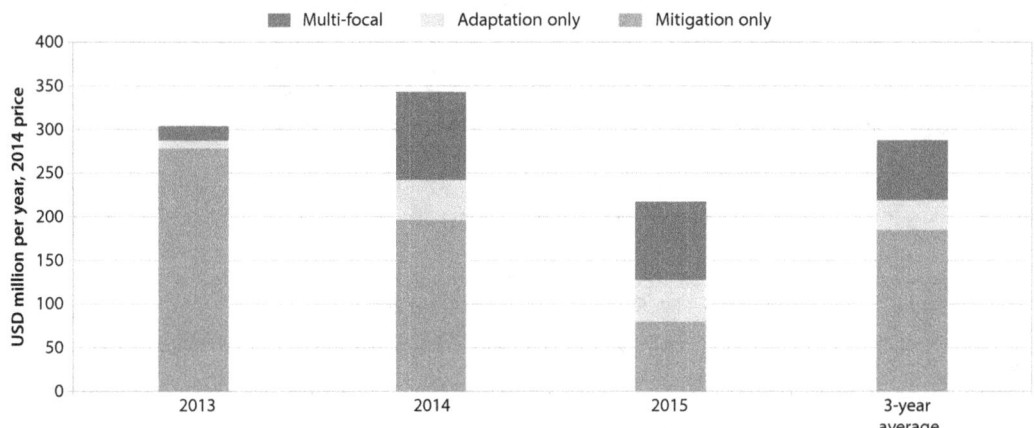

Notes: 1. Total climate-related development finance equals mitigation only + adaptation only – multi-focal. Multi-focal projects mean that their focus includes both mitigation and adaptation.

2. The size of the finance is the amount committed, but not necessarily disbursed, by providers.

Source: Author's analysis based on OECD (2017c), Climate-related development finance data at the activity level reported to the OECD DAC Creditors Reporting System (CRS), www.oecd.org/dac/stats/climate-change.htm.

Figure 4.3 shows that multilateral and bilateral providers of development finance committed about USD 863 million of climate-related development finance over 2013-15 (USD 287 million per year) for mitigation and adaptation in Georgia. Of this amount, 28.5% of mitigation finance and 47.4% of multi-focal (i.e. mitigation and adaptation) finance were committed to hydropower projects.

The fluctuations in the annual committed amounts can be attributed to a few large-scale projects. For instance, the hike in the amount in 2014 is partly due to a large-scale project for the Shuakhevi hydropower station construction. This multi-focal (mitigation and adaptation) project, supported by EBRD, amounted to USD 97.5 million in 2014. In 2013, Germany committed USD 94.6 million towards a project to enhance the electricity transmission capacities, strengthen security and quality of the electricity supply, and promote the network connection of renewable energies, especially in hydropower.

The European neighbourhood programme for agriculture and rural development Phase 2 (ENPARD II) is another large-scale multi-focal project. The European Union committed USD 65.6 million to this project in 2015. It aims to enhance food production and income in Georgia and reduce rural poverty, while addressing climate-related risks to these sectors.

Attracting private-sector investment in adaptation is more difficult than for mitigation in general. As a result, the role of development finance in filling the adaptation finance gap is important (Pauw, 2015). It is encouraging that the share of adaptation and multi-focal (i.e. adaptation and mitigation) projects in total committed amount increased over 2013-15 (Figure 4.3.). Nevertheless, data show that the commitment of climate-related development finance to mitigation projects still outweighs adaptation finance in the same three-year period. Specifically, mitigation-only projects received 64% of finance, while adaptation-only projects received 12%, and multi-focal projects received 24%.

In middle-income countries, including Georgia, development finance is increasingly expected to catalyse private-sector investment rather than provide large amounts of concessional finance. Such catalytic effect would be best performed if support is aligned with the needs of the private sector entities active in the country. Development finance institutions often take a blended approach. This involves strategic use of grants and commercial-term financial resources to, for instance, support households, enterprises and farmers with taking up energy efficiency and renewable measures. The draft Low Emission Development Strategy (LEDS) suggests better use of blended finance as a way to mobilise investment to achieve low-carbon development.

Development financial institutions have extended credit lines to local commercial banks and microfinance institutions for energy-efficiency activities in households and at corporations, as well as renewable energy projects in recent years (Table 4.3). In middle-income countries, deploying such on-lent environmental credit lines through local financial institutions is a relatively well-established way of supporting green investment, including in Georgia. These programmes often consist of loan finance for purchasing energy-efficient goods or renewable energy equipment, as well as grants for technical assistance to select and use/operate such products and services.

With the support of development finance institutions, local banks in such countries can offer loans for renewable energy and energy efficiency at lower interest rates than the market. However, the reduced interest rates may not always be low enough for customers to take the loan. Lending is also often hampered by different factors. These include lack of information on investment opportunities and an insufficient level of technological maturity of certain climate-related projects. Other barriers include high collateral requirements and/or additional charges for various transaction costs (e.g. operations and overhead, currency swap fees) and risks (e.g. currency and political risks).

Development finance institutions also play an important role in bridging the knowledge gap. They test relatively new financial solutions that target a variety of climate- and energy-related issues and risks in Georgia. These institutions also help local financial institutions adopt better management systems that can facilitate investment or lending directed to climate-related projects. For instance, DEG (the German Investment and Development Company – a subsidiary of KfW) has worked with JSC TBC Bank to enable the bank to adopt and implement a formal Environmental and Social Management System (ESMS). The ESMS includes a specific exclusion list to screen project proposals, the appointment of a dedicated Environmental and Social Officer and an annual report on environment and social performance. A third-party assessment has concluded that TBC Bank is implementing the ESMS to a high standard, ensuring buy-in from loan officers and strong commitment by the bank's senior management (Citrus Partners, 2016).

Country ownership over accessing and managing development finance to maximise the effectiveness of development co-operation has long been discussed (e.g. OECD-DAC, 2005). It is extremely important for the government of Georgia. For example, it can support decisions on project priorities. It can also help implementation and monitoring of selected projects in light of the various strategic documents on climate change and green growth.

One of the Green Climate Fund (GCF)'s primary goals is to enhance country ownership. Consequently, the government of Georgia and GIZ work on "Readiness" programme to access funding from the GCF. The programme seeks to set up institutional structures for co-ordinated engagement with the GCF (i.e. a climate finance co-ordination mechanism) and for issuance of no-objection letters. The Readiness activities also support design and implementation of the national dialogue process. This promotes prioritisation of project proposals and elaboration of the concept notes of these projects. This Readiness programme is financially supported by the GCF.

As of 2017, JSC Partnership Fund, JSC TBC Bank and the Georgian government also work on "direct access" to the funding resources of the GCF, as discussed in section 4.1.2. International entities play an important role in delivering climate finance. However, the country may benefit from pursuing direct access to improve efficiency (e.g. reducing

Table 4.3. **Examples of credit line programmes by development financial institutions related to energy efficiency and renewable energy**

Programme	Debt provider	Grant provider	Local institutions	Focus	Signed/Approved
Energocredit	EBRD	EU (NIF), Austria, EBRD	Bank of Georgia, TBC Bank, BASIS Bank, CREDO Bank, VTB	EE and RE	2014
FMO-Crystal Local currency loan (partly for green investment)	FMO	n.a.	Microfinance Organisation Crystal	EE and RE	2017
GCF-EBRD Sustainable Energy Financing Facilities	EBRD	GCF, EBRD, KTFC	tbd	EE and RE	2016
GCPF-TBC Bank climate loan facility	GCPF	n.a.	TBC Bank	Primarily in RE (small hydro)	2016
GGF credit line for energy efficiency and renewable energy	GGF (EIB, EBRD, KfW, FMO and OeEB)	GGF (Germany, OeEB and EU)	Bank of Georgia, TBC Bank	EE and RE	2014, 2015
GGF credit line for energy-efficient housing	GGF (EIB, EBRD, KfW, IFC, FMO and OeEB)	GGF (Germany, OeEB and EU)	m2 Real Estate	EE	2015
KfW Facility for Promotion of Renewable Energies	KfW	OeEB	Bank of Georgia	RE (Hydro)	2012
SME Energy and Environment loans/ Loan for SMEs and Mid-caps	EIB	n.a.	Bank of Georgia, TBC Bank, Procredit Bank	Supporting SMEs and mid-caps in various fields including EE and RE.	2011-16
(DCFTA SME Facility)	EBRD	EU (NIF)	Bank of Georgia, TBC Bank	Despite the primary focus being support for SMEs in exporting goods to EU markets, the major part can go to EE	2017

DCFTA: Deep and Comprehensive Free Trade Area, **EBRD**: European Bank for Reconstruction and Development, **EIB**: European Investment Bank, **FMO**: Dutch Development Bank, **GCF**: Green Climate Fund, **GCPF**: Global Climate Partnership Fund, **GGF**: Green for Growth Fund, **IFC**: International Finance Corporation, **KTCF**: Korea Technical Assistance and Cooperation Fund, **NIF**: EC Neighbourhood Investment Facility, **n.a.**: Information not available, **OeEB**: Austrian Development Bank.

Source: Author's analysis based on Bank of Georgia (2014), TBC Bank (2015), Energocredit (2016), GCF (n.d.), FMO (2017) and GCFP (2017).

transaction costs). It could also strengthen ownership over accessing and better using green finance from international sources. Nevertheless, direct access and access through international entities to GCF resources should co-exist and complement each other. Indeed, Georgia and its development co-operation partners are actively engaging with the GCF. The GCF Board has approved two projects that will partly be implemented in Georgia: the GCF-EBRD Sustainable Energy Financing Facilities and GEEREF NeXt with the EIB (GCF, n.d.).

Exploring new financial channels for green finance

Using a broader range of financial instruments than collateral lending would help lower financial cost and complement commercial bank loans. This, in turn, would scale up finance for climate action in Georgia over time (MoESD, 2016; OECD, 2017a, 2017b). The market capitalisation ratio of listed companies to GDP in Georgia was around 7% in 2014. This is low compared to, for instance, the low- and middle-income Europe and Central Asian countries (19.5%) and the European Union (52%) (World Bank, 2017). The Capital Market Development Strategy developed by the government of Georgia and the National Bank of Georgia (the central bank) also aims to decrease the dominance of commercial banks (MoESD, 2016).

The Global Energy Efficiency and Renewable Energy Fund (GEEREF), advised by the European Investment Bank (EIB) Group, was launched in 2008 as a public-private investment vehicle. It aims to provide equity financing for the development of small and medium-sized renewable energy and energy-efficiency projects across emerging markets and economies in transition. Among its investments, GEEREF has committed USD 13 million to an equity fund called Caucasus Clean Energy Fund (CCEF). It supports development of small and medium-sized hydropower plants in Georgia through risk capital, technical expertise, and provision of best environmental and social practices. Managed by the private-sector fund manager, Schulze Global Investments Limited, the CCEF has received additional commitments up to USD 50 million from other foreign investors and the JSC Partnership Fund. The CCEF targets 10-20 MW hydropower plants.

Equity financing for companies or projects that contribute to improved energy efficiency seems to be perceived as riskier, low-return investments in Georgia, thus often needs concessional capitals backed by (international) development financial institutions or sovereign funds (Singh et al., 2016). Non-bank financing channels, such as leasing, vendor credits and private-sector energy service companies are limited as financial sources for energy efficiency in Georgia. Still, they have potential to improve risk-return profiles of energy-efficiency activities and projects (Chernyavskay and van Waveren Horgervorst, 2017).

Green bonds are attracting more interest in Georgia (Van Bilsen, 2017), and the government or Georgian corporations could consider issuing green sovereign or corporate bonds. Georgia faces several major challenges, such as scalability of projects and the nascent bond market. However, green bonds still have potential to lower financing and re-financing costs of green investment in corporations and projects (OECD, 2017b). The government and some large Georgian companies have already issued sovereign and corporate bonds (see Chapter 5.1). These could be a good foundation for future issuance of green bonds. Georgia would also need to develop its green bond standard or adopt an existing one(s) developed by other institutions or countries. Existing standards include the Green Bonds Principles, the Climate Bonds Standards and the Green Financial Bond Directive by the People's Bank of China.

Bond finance could benefit Georgia's effort for scaling up investments in climate-related projects (especially infrastructure) over time in the following ways (see also Box 4.3):

- helping raise capital directly for climate-related projects, or refinance existing shorter-term loans potentially at a lower cost

- providing greater flexibility and more options to free up early project phase capital after it has been deployed, as well as for the longer-term project finance debt held by banks constrained by deleveraging and regulations ("recycling of capital")

- enabling financial institutions to use bonds to resolve maturity mismatches between loans and liabilities (OECD, 2017b).

Box 4.3. **Different types of green bonds**

Green bonds could take several forms. OECD (2017b) outlines several different forms and discusses their characteristics. These different forms of green bonds, which could potentially be used for climate action in Georgia, are listed below.

1. **Corporate bond** is a "use of proceeds" bond issued by a corporate entity with recourse to the issuer in the case of default on interest payments or on return of principal. As a sub-category, the financial sector bond is issued by a financial institution to raise capital specifically to finance "on-balance sheet lending" (i.e. to provide loans) to green activities (e.g. ABN AMRO or Agricultural Bank of China).

2. **Project bond** is a bond backed by single or multiple projects for which the investor has direct exposure to the risk of the project, with or without recourse to the bond issuer.

3. **Asset-backed security (ABS)** is a bond collateralised by one or more specific projects, usually providing recourse only to the assets, except in the case of covered bonds (included in this category). For covered bonds, the primary recourse is to the issuing entity, with secondary recourse to an underlying cover pool of assets, in the event of default of the issuer.

4. **Supranational, sub-sovereign and agency (SSA) bonds** are those issued by development finance institutions such as the World Bank and the European Investment Bank (i.e. "supranational issuers"). SSA bonds and corporate bonds both have features relating to "use of proceeds" and recourse to the issuer. Agency bonds are included in this category (e.g. issuance by export-import banks), as are sub-sovereign national development banks (e.g. the German KfW).

5. **Sovereign bond** is issued by a national government. Poland issued the first sovereign green bond in December 2016, followed by France in January 2017. Several other countries have indicated their intention to issue sovereign green bonds.

6. **Municipal bond** is issued by a municipal government, region or city.

Source: Based on OECD (2017b).

To help "demonstration issuance" of green bonds, development finance institutions could provide cornerstone investments in Georgia. For instance, Georgia is a target country of the IFC's Green Bond Cornerstone Program. This is a platform to invest in green bonds issued by financial institutions active in developing countries. Further, as an example from outside of Georgia, the inaugural green bonds in India, issued by Yes Bank, were supported by IFC. Yes Bank is meant to invest the proceeds of the bonds in renewable energy and energy-efficiency projects, mainly in the solar and wind sector (IFC, 2015). In another example from outside of Georgia, the GCF and the Inter-American Development Bank support Colombia, the Dominican Republic, Jamaica and Mexico. Their aggregating energy-efficiency projects underpin the issuance of partly guaranteed green bonds (IDB, 2015). It would be worth considering replication of such a programme in Georgia.

The current Budget Code of Georgia does not allow specific revenues to be allocated or earmarked for specific purposes, including climate-related activities. Potentially, municipal bonds could be issued to finance climate-related projects at the sub-national level. However, this would likely require a careful review of the municipalities' creditworthiness to ensure soundness of the bond market.

In terms of capital sources, Georgian microfinance institutions can play a greater role in financing Georgia's climate action in the future. Some institutions are starting to see it as a potential business opportunity. They foresee building on their extensive networks from big cities to small rural villages, as well as on their deep knowledge about their borrowers' circumstances. Microfinance is, however, likely to need concessional financing to lower its high interest rates. It needs to match typical characteristics of energy-efficiency activities and decentralised renewable energy, for example, with long payback periods and greater levels of technical uncertainty. For instance, Microfinance Organization (MFO) Crystal and the Dutch Development Bank, FMO, reached a USD 10-million loan agreement. They plan to disburse USD 1 million as green finance (See Box 4.4).

Box 4.4. **Microfinance Organization Crystal's Green Funding Action Plan**

Microfinance Organization (MFO) Crystal has developed its Green Funding Action Plan through the engagement of a broad range of stakeholders such as potential partners, and consultants from the private, public and academic sectors. MFO Crystal has reviewed its loan portfolio for environmental considerations. It has also developed a list of possible projects such as energy efficiency, renewable (e.g. rooftop solar and biofuels), sustainable tourism, water supply and sanitation, and sustainable agriculture, some of which are outlined as follows:

- replacing heat supply systems
- insulating outside walls
- replacing outside doors and windows with energy-efficient ones
- adopting thermal solar systems
- replacing mini tractors
- adopting drip irrigation systems
- adopting energy-efficient home appliances such as refrigerators, washing machines, dishwasher, ovens and air conditioning systems.

Source: MFO Crystal (2017).

Developing an institutional investor base could also help Georgia mobilise finance for actions to achieve its goals on climate change and green growth over time. This base could take the form of pension funds, banks, insurance companies, equity funds, real estate investment trusts, investment advisors and mutual funds. Some equity funds (the Partnership Fund, the Georgian Energy Development Fund, and the Georgia Co-Investment

Fund) already invest in energy, healthcare, real estate, tourism and manufacturing. The same is true for subsidiaries of the large financial groups such as BGEO Group PLC (BGEO Group, 2017). However, there is still much room to enhance mainstreaming climate or green aspects into their portfolios.

Georgia is also reforming its pension system (Schwarz et al., 2016). This could potentially be a future source of funding for climate-related projects through direct investment or purchase of green bonds. It is not yet clear whether such climate-related projects or bonds can be an eligible asset class for Georgia pension funds. The Ministry of Finance and the Ministry of Economy and Sustainable Development estimate that the accumulation of pension fund assets will increase from GEL 313 million (USD 128.8 million) in 2018 to GEL 29.7 billion (USD 12.2 billion) in 2035 (Paresishvili, 2017). The Georgian Stock Exchange expects such pension fund assets to be a significant funding source for the domestic economy through debt and equity financing (Paresishvili, 2017). Another study stresses the need for diversified asset allocation rather than over-investment in bonds, as well as sensible investment regulations on pension funds in Georgia (Schwarz et al., 2016).

References

Agenda.GE. (22 June 2017), "Shares of Georgia's wind farm to be sold at Georgian Stock Exchange", Agenda.GE News blog, http://agenda.ge/news/81955/eng (accessed 30 October 2017).

Bank of Georgia (2014), *Bank of Georgia: Green Project Financing*, JSC Bank of Georgia, Tbilisi, https://www.oecd.org/env/outreach/2_5_Private-bank-perspective.pdf (accessed 30 October 2017).

BGEO Group (2017), *BGEO Group PLC Annual Report 2016*, BGEO Group, London, www.bgeo.com.

Caucasus Business Week (28 November 2016), "More oxygen in city – Electric vehicles infrastructure to appear in Tbilisi, Batumi and Kutaisi – CBW.ge", Georgia News blog, http://cbw.ge/georgia/oxygen-city-electric-vehicles-infrastructure-appear-tbilisi-batumi-kutaisi/ (accessed 30 October 2017).

Chernyavskay, T. and M. van Waveren Horgervorst (2017), "Financing RECP measures at SMEs: An overlooked opportunity", presentation at International Conference: Unlocking Private Finance for Energy Efficiency and Greener, Low-Carbon Growth in the Eastern Partnership and Central Asia Countries, 30 June 2017, https://www.slideshare.net/OECD_ENV/session-4-presentation-by-tatiana-chernyavskaya-and-marko-van-waveren-unido (accessed 30 October 2017).

Citrus Partners (2016), *Evaluation of the Promotion of Environmental and Social Standards in DEG's Indirect Financing Case Study Report – TBC Bank, Georgia*, Citrus Partners, London, https://www.deginvest.de/DEG-Documents-in-English/About-us/What-is-our-impact/E-S-Study2017-TBC-Bank-Europe-Georgia.pdf (accessed 30 October 2017).

Copenhagen Centre on Energy Efficiency (2017), *Energy Efficiency Brief: Tbilisi, Georgia*, Copenhagen Centre on Energy Efficiency, http://kms.energyefficiencycentre.org/publication-report/energy-efficiency-brief-tbilisi-georgia.

EIB (2016), *Georgia: Neighbourhood SME Financing*, European Investment Bank, Luxembourg, www.eib.org/attachments/efs/economic_report_neighbourhood_sme_financing_georgia_en.pdf.

Energocredit (2016), Energocredit Georgia website, http://energocredit.ge/en (accessed 13 October 2017).

FMO (2017), "Project Detail: MFO Crystal – FMO", webpage, https://www.fmo.nl/project-detail/51156 (accessed 13 October 2017).

Galt & Taggart (2016), *Georgia's Energy Sector Electricity Market Watch*, Galt & Taggart Research, Tbilisi.

GCF (n.d.), "Projects + Programmes", Green Climate Fund, www.greenclimate.fund/what-we-do/projects-programmes (accessed 13 October 2017).

GCFP (2017), "GCPF and TBC Bank, Georgia, agree on USD 25 million climate loan facility – Global Climate Partnership Fund", Press Release, 2 February 2017, Global Climate Partnership Fund, London, https://www.gcpf.lu/press-release-detail/gcpf-and-tbc-bank-georgia-agree-on-usd-25-million-climate-loan-facility.html.

GEDF (18 January 2017), "Georgian Energy Development Fund announces selection of investor for development of Zestaponi WPP project", Georgian Energy Development Fund, Investors blog, http://gedf.com.ge/en/georgian-energy-development-fund-announces-selection-of-investor-for-devepolment-of-zestaponi-wpp-project/ (accessed 30 October 2017).

Georgian Co-Investment Fund (2014), *GCFUND – Mtkvari HPP*, Georgian Co-Investment Fund, Tbilisi, http://gcfund.ge/en/energyandinfrastructure/5/ (accessed 30 October 2017).

IDB (2015), "Consideration of funding proposals – Addendum funding proposal summary for FP006: Energy efficiency green nonds in Latin America and the Caribbean", Inter-American Development Bank (IDB), Washington, DC, https://www.greenclimate.fund/documents/20182/87610/GCF_B.11_04_ADD.06_-_Funding_proposal_package_for_FP006.pdf/4be31e42-bda9-46a0-b200-bc2f78ed81d6.

IFC (2015), "IFC issues first Green Masala bond", *News Release*, August 2015, www.ifc.org/wps/wcm/connect/news_ext_content/ifc_external_corporate_site/news+and+events/news/ifc+issues+first+green+masala+bond+on+london+stock+exchange.

IMF (2017) Investment and Capital Stock Dataset 1960-2015 (January 2017 version), www.imf.org/external/np/fad/publicinvestment/ (accessed 06 November 2017).

Masullo, I. et al. (2015). "Direct access to climate finance: Lessons learned by national institutions", *Working Paper*, World Resources Institute, Washington, DC, https://www.wri.org/sites/default/files/22DIRECT_ACCESS_TO_CLIMATE_FINANCE_LESSONS_LEARNED_BY_NATIONAL_INSTITUTIONS.pdf.

MFO Crystal (30 July 2017), "Crystal's green funding strategy workshop", Microfinance Organization Crystal News blog, http://crystal.ge/en/news/549/. (accessed 30 October 2017).

MoESD (2016), *Capital Market Development Strategy*, Ministry of Economy and Sustainable Development with the Ministry of Finance and the National Bank of Georgia, Tbilisi.

National Bank of Georgia (2017), *Key Macroeconomic Indicators and International Ratings, 2011-16*, https://www.nbg.gov.ge/index.php?m=494. (accessed 30 October 2017).

National Bank of Georgia (2016), *Georgian Banking Sector and Some Opportunities in Non-banking Financial Sector*, National Bank of Georgia, Tbilisi, https://www.nbg.gov.ge/uploads/publications/on/f/Georgian%20Banking%20Sector%20-%20short%20overview.pdf.

OECD (2017a), *Investing in Climate, Investing in Growth*, OECD Publishing, Paris, http://dx.doi.org/10.1787/9789264273528-en.

OECD (2017b), *Mobilising Bond Markets for a Low-Carbon Transition*, OECD Publishing, Paris, http://dx.doi.org/10.1787/9789264272323-en.

OECD (2017c), *Climate-related development finance data at the activity level reported to the OECD DAC Creditors Reporting System (CRS)*, www.oecd.org/dac/stats/climate-change.htm (acessed 30 October 2017).

OECD (2016), *Financing Climate Action in Eastern Europe, the Caucasus and Central Asia*, OECD Publishing, Paris, http://dx.doi.org/10.1787/9789264266339-en.

OECD (2015), *Infrastructure Financing Instruments and Incentives*, OECD Publishing, Paris, www.oecd.org/finance/private-pensions/Infrastructure-Financing-Instruments-and-Incentives.pdf.

OECD-DAC (2005), *The Paris Declaration on Aid Effectiveness and the Accra Agenda for Action*, OECD Development Assistance Committee (DAC), Paris, www.oecd.org/dac/effectiveness/34428351.pdf.

Paresishvili, G. (2017), *Georgian Stock Exchange: Georgian Capital Market Development*, https://www.saras.gov.ge/Content/files/GSE-Capital-Market-Development-FINAL-ENG-19.06.17.pdf.

Partnership Fund (14 June 2016), "Partnership Fund launches Ytong energy efficient block factory project", JSC Partnership Fund News and Media blog, www.fund.ge/eng/view_news/736. (accessed 30 October 2017).

Pauw, W. (2015), "Not a panacea: Private-sector engagement in adaptation and adaptation finance in developing countries", *Climate Policy*, Vol. 15/5, Taylor & Francis Online, pp. 583-606, http://dx.doi.org/:10.1080/14693062.2014.953906.

ProCredit Bank Georgia (2017), *Green Finance Development*, presentation at policy dialogue on green economy in Georgia – workshop on green finance mobilisation in Tbilisi, 22-23 June 2017. https://www.slideshare.net/OECD_ENV/session-6-presentation-by-procredit-bank-georgia.

Schwarz, A. et al. (2016), "Pension reform in Georgia", www.economy.ge/uploads/meniu_publikaciebi/ouer/msoplio_bankis_prezentacia.pdf (acessed 30 October 2017).

Singh, J. et al. (2016), *Energy Efficiency Financing Option Papers for Georgia*, World Bank, Washington, DC, http://documents.worldbank.org/curated/en/825761475845097689/Energy-efficiency-financing-option-papers-for-Georgia.

Tan, C. and M. Dolidze (2017), *Georgia – Public Expenditure Review :Building a Sustainable Future*, World Bank, Washington, DC, http://documents.worldbank.org/curated/en/630321497350151165/Georgia-Public-expenditure-review-building-a-sustainable-future.

TBC Bank (2015), "TBC bank signs two subordinated loan agreements for USD 30 million from EFSE and GGF", *Press Release*, 7 December 2015, http://irtest.tbcbank.ge/?site-lang=en&site-path=news/press/&type=2&now=1&id=501&site-session=89424087df001a584057122a0d109cc9 (accessed 30 October 2017).

Van Bilsen, J. (16 January 2017), "Green Bond Market in Georgia – a Growing Opportunity", Georgia Today on the Web News blog, http://georgiatoday.ge/news/5609/Green-Bond-Market-in-Georgia-%E2%80%93-a-Growing-Opportunity (accessed 30 October 2017).

World Bank (2017), *World Development Indicators*, World Bank Group, Washington, DC, http://wdi.worldbank.org/tables (accessed 31 October 2017).

World Bank (2015), "Absorbing external shocks", *Georgia Economic Update*, No. 2, Fall 2015, World Bank Group, Washington, DC, https://openknowledge.worldbank.org/bitstream/handle/10986/23598/Georgia000Absorbing0external0shocks.pdf?sequence=1.

WTO (2015), *Trade Policy Review: Georgia*, World Trade Organization, Geneva, https://www.wto.org/english/tratop_e/tpr_e/s328_e.pdf.

Chapter 5

Aligning broader enabling conditions for investments with Georgia's climate action

Scaling up finance for climate action in Georgia requires a broader set of conditions that enable further finance to flow to achieve the country's long-term goals. This chapter reviews a range of policies that directly or indirectly influence investment conditions to mobilise such finance in Georgia. It examines enabling conditions on the following areas: financial market design; provision of risk mitigation instruments; public funding entities, and competition (especially in the electricity sector). The chapter also briefly discusses gaps in information, awareness and capacity, and potential options to bridge them. Filling these gaps is also an important enabling condition on both demand and supply sides of finance.

Financial market policies

Developing a well-functioning capital market has great potential to complement bank lending, diversify financial channels and lower the cost of investment. In so doing, it enhances the flow of capital, including for climate action, in Georgia (MoESD, 2016; OECD, 2017a, 2017b). The government (including state-owned utility companies), development finance institutions and commercial banks will continue to be an important source of direct investment in, and on-lending to, climate-related projects in the country. However, the scale of finance ultimately needed to achieve climate-related goals is large. Further, there is a maturity mismatch between short-term funding and the long-term payback period of assets. As a result, the finance needed is likely to exceed the capacity of these sources. The government's fiscal space is limited. Development finance institutions alone cannot meet the financial demand for Georgia's climate action and are supposed to avoid crowding out private-sector finance. Moreover, commercial banks face challenges in accessing and providing low-cost, long-tenor loans.

Current issues: High interest rates, collateral requirement and dollarisation

Availability of long-term and low-cost financial resources and increasing accumulation of government debt are major concerns for scaling up investments. This is true for climate-related projects, but also for nearly all sorts of fixed assets in Georgia. Georgian businesses consider the high interest rates on commercial bank lending to be one of the biggest obstacles to mobilising climate-related investment (Figure 5.1). Interest rates on commercial bank lending are particularly high in the national currency, Georgian Lari (GEL) (17.3% in August 2017) compared to foreign currency loans (9.1%) (National Bank of Georgia, 2017a).

Figure 5.1. **Interests rates in Georgia**

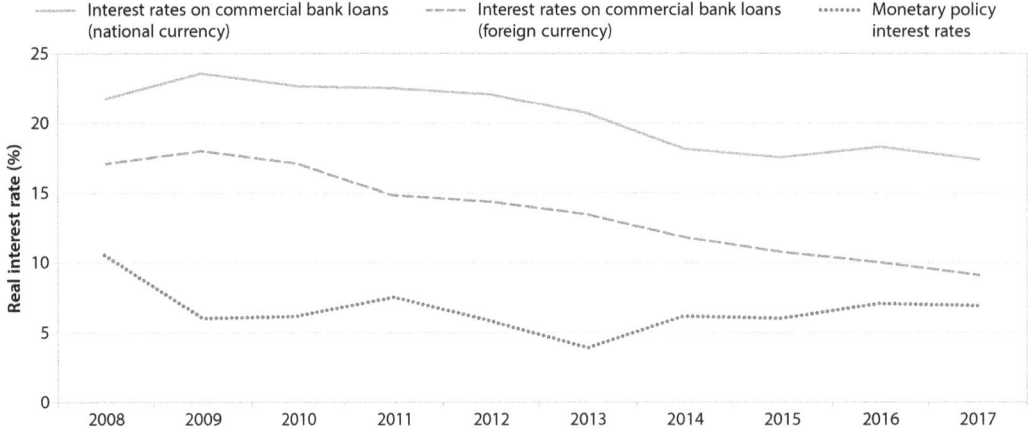

Source: Based on National Bank of Georgia (2017a).

Studies suggest several energy-efficiency measures are available at or below net zero costs in the long run in Georgia (Wing and Timilsina, 2016). However, the limited availability of long-term capital results in the maturity mismatches between such measures and available finance. Lowering the cost of capital is also important for renewable energy. The financial cost of capital represents about 50-70% of the costs of electricity generation (OECD, 2017b).

Many Georgian commercial banks tend to be reluctant to lower interest rates. They often lack sufficient knowledge and information on actual risks, as well as technical specifications of green investments. This is true even for the relatively well-established technologies such as hydropower (e.g. hydrological and engineering parameters and related performance). The National Bank of Georgia has held its benchmark monetary interest rate at 7% as of July 2017 (Figure 5.1); the annual inflation rate in 2017 (6.0% as of July) is higher than its 4% target during the year (National Bank of Georgia, 2017a). This also influences the persistently high commercial bank interest rates especially in national currency.

The government needs to address issues around high interest rates, while promoting climate action. To that end, the government the government could integrate climate-related criteria into its existing support programmes for small- and medium-sized enterprises (SMEs). The government already provides targeted interest rate subsidies through the Enterprise Georgia and the Agricultural Project Management Agency. Care should be taken to ensure that such support should not hamper more general climate- and environment-related policies and regulations.

The high collateral requirement from banks (about 220% of the value of the loan) also makes it difficult for Georgian companies to take loans (EIB, 2016; EU4Business, 2017). This is particularly an issue for SMEs since they often do not have sufficient collateral. According to Georgian banking regulations, commercial banks cannot expose more than 25% of assets in their total portfolio to uncollateralised loans. However, banks normally do not reach this threshold. This implies that the level of commercial banks' risk aversion is likely to be greater than that required by regulations (EIB, 2016). Leasing could help solve issues associated with collateral requirements since it requires no collateral and generally has more flexible pay-back schedules. However, the lease market in Georgia is still at the very early stage of development, thus largely underused (EIB, 2016; Chernyavskay and van Waveren Horgervorst, 2017).

The country credit rating for Georgia remains relatively low, albeit stable (e.g. Fitch: BB+, Moody's: Ba3, S&P: BB-) (National Bank of Georgia, 2017b). This also contributes to high interest rates and a drive towards short tenors of available capital. Perceived country risks of Georgia may not always reflect a real risk, but seem to influence the country credit rating. Perceived risks also make it more difficult to find funding partners, especially from overseas, for structuring green finance projects. Recent economic and political situations of Georgia are considered stable: the currency volatility and inflation rate are largely within targets set by the National Bank of Georgia (NBG). Nevertheless, Georgia has a relatively small-scale economy and population. The economic and political circumstances of neighbours often affect Georgia's credit rating. For instance, the recent economic crisis in Turkey and the Russian Federation led to negative impacts on Georgia's economy, such as a decline in export of electricity and Georgian products.

A high degree of dollarisation of assets in Georgia may also have various implications for mobilising finance for climate action. In addition, it could have various negative effects on the country's fiscal sustainability and the effectiveness of monetary policies in general. The dollarisation also tends to cause currency-induced credit risks if the currency depreciates as occurred in 2015. Roughly 65% of deposits and loans are in US dollars; over 90% of foreign currency borrowers rely on income in GEL (EIB, 2016). The government of Georgia and NBG launched a programme that encourages borrowers to convert USD-denominated loans to GEL with a preferential exchange rate. It allows loans in small amounts (up to GEL 100 000) to be only issued in GEL (National Bank of Georgia, 2016).

Looking at Georgia's capital market development through a green finance lens

Georgia's capital market (especially for corporate bonds and equity) is still at an early stage of development. A working group, hosted by the Georgian government with support of the Asian Development Bank, pointed out that underdevelopment of Georgia's capital market resulted from multiple events and policy choices over the past. The global financial crisis and the war against the Russian Federation in 2008, for example, undermined momentum for developing the financial market. Furthermore, in 2007-08, the country made a set of radical amendments to the Law on Securities Market of Georgia in light of market liberalisation. This has further decreased transparency of the securities trading markets (Capital Markets Working Group, 2015).

The Ministry of Economy and Sustainable Development, Ministry of Finance and NBG prepared a draft report on the Capital Market Development Strategy in 2016. The report stresses that "Capital Market, in parallel with the banking lending, is considered as an effective facility for attracting financial resources" and "deep, transparent and well-regulated capital markets contribute to stable growth and economy and people's welfare" (MoESD, 2016). The Ministry of Economy and Sustainable Development, the Ministry of Finance and NBG are carrying out a series of legislative reforms for capital market development, financial education and infrastructure development (e.g. the payment system).

Capital market reforms in Georgia are also an opportunity to make the financial sector conducive to green finance mobilisation. The government and NBG have been reviewing the diverse range of laws relating to financial sector regulations. These include laws on securities markets, investment funds, entrepreneurs, and accounting and financial audit. Aspects related to climate or green growth have not yet become part of this work. However, actors working on financial market development have shown growing interest in this issue at several forums (e.g. OECD, 2017c; Van Bilsen, 2017).

In Georgia, neither equity nor corporate bond is commonly used as a financial instrument in general, let alone as finance for climate action. The exception is for equity investments in hydropower projects and a few wind power projects (e.g. Qartli Wind Farm). Nevertheless, there are emerging examples of Georgian corporations that have recently issued bonds in the Georgian Stock Exchange. Others have issued bonds outside of the country such as in the London Stock Exchange and the Irish Stock Exchange (Table 5.1). JSC Bank of Georgia, for example, issued its first local currency corporate bonds with support

Table 5.1. **Examples of issued bonds and their performance**

	Sector	Currency	Size (million)	Maturity	Coupon	Exchange	Rating (Fitch)
Government of Georgia	Government	USD	500	2021	6.88	London	BB-
Georgian Oil & Gas Corp	Energy	USD	250	2021	6.75	London	BB-
BGEO Group	Financial	USD	350	2023	6.00	Irish	BB-
Bank of Georgia	Financial	GEL	500	2020	11.00	Irish	BB-
Georgian Railway	Industrial	USD	500	2022	7.75	London	B+
Georgian Leasing Co	Financial	USD	10	2017	8.75	Georgia	-
M2 Real Estate	Real Estate	USD	25	2019	7.50	Georgia	-
Nikora Trade	Retail	USD	5	2018	11.00	Georgia	-
Georgian Water & Power	Utilities	GEL	30	2021	11.25	Not listed	BB-
Georgian Water & Power	Utilities	GEL	2.6	2017	14.00	Georgia	BB-

GEL: Georgian Laris.
Source: Adopted from Galt & Taggart (2017) and JSC Bank of Georgia (2017).

of IFC. This attracted approximately USD 200 million from about 20 international investors (JSC Bank of Georgia, 2017). To support the bonds market, some development finance institutions have issued bonds denominated by the local currency GEL. The European Bank for Reconstruction and Development, for example, issued GEL-denominated Eurobonds under its Global Medium-Term Note Programme (Martikian, 2017).

Table 5.2 illustrates that Georgia is taking steady steps to improve the financial market. Affected areas include bond issuance, credit rating services, payment services and financial education. The government and the NBG generally support the idea of "greening" the Georgian financial system. However, Table 5.2 shows formal discussions have not yet begun on introducing "green" elements or any environment, society and governance factors into the financial system. Even if the reforms lack an explicitly "green" mandate, improving the Georgian capital market will likely have positive direct and indirect implications for future green finance mobilisation.

Table 5.2. **Key factors for developing Georgia's capital market and its status**

Key factors for developing "green" capital markets	Status in Georgia
Well-functioning local capital market	Under development: Government bonds and other major corporate bonds have been issued, but are still a small fraction of the total financial asset and issued outside Georgia.
Credit rating services	NBG and Fitch Ratings started a pilot credit rating service for major Georgian companies, including the largest commercial banks.
Good payment service	NBG's clearing and settlement system development is being finalised as of 2017.
Government yield curve	Government GEL bond yield curve was introduced in 2015.
Financial education	The National Strategy for Financial Education was adopted in 2016.
Measures to promote ESG* performance of assets	Not yet considered.
Green bond guideline and standards	Not yet considered.

ESG: Environment, Social and Governance; **GEL**: Georgian Lari; **NBG**: National Bank of Georgia.

Source: Author's analysis.

Making best use of risk mitigation instruments

Georgia has used various instruments to mitigate political, macroeconomic, regulatory, business and technical risks. These include credit enhancement mechanisms and direct public investment (Table 5.3). Reforming the capital market is essential, but takes a long time. Such instruments are therefore powerful tools to create market-based incentives for commercial banks, equity investors and other types of financial institutions. They allow scaling up of investment in climate-related projects and activities in Georgia in a relatively short time. Reduced risk is also expected to encourage financial institutions, such as commercial banks, to lower collateral requirements and interest rates for their clients. Tax reduction, interest subsidies and credit guarantees can also be used for specific financial products such as a future issuance of green bonds.

As mentioned earlier, investors have already seen hydropower projects in Georgia as a bankable asset class. However, these projects are made possible by the government's revenue guarantees through fixed tariffs under power purchase agreements (PPAs), as well as other preferential policies (e.g. priority access to the electricity grid and VAT exemptions). PPAs enhance credit, ensuring long-term revenues to renewable projects in the country. The government is revising the associated rules to allow individual tariff/price level for each project.

Table 5.3. **Examples of risk mitigation instruments**

Category	Instrument	Description	Examples from Georgia
Credit enhancement	Revenue guarantee	Guaranteeing certain cash flows for a project, such as through regulated tariffs	Each project agrees on a power purchase agreement backed by the government (currently with a capped tariff: 6 US cents/kWh for less than eight months a year).
	Layered fund subordination	Taking a subordinated position in a fund to give priority to private investors for claims on assets	The Green for Growth Fund created a USD 15 million subordinated loan facility with TBC Bank to expand funding for energy efficiency and renewable energy projects.
	(Partial) credit guarantee	Guaranteeing payments for the principal and interest on debt issuance (up to a certain percentage) under new or existing loan portfolios in the event of non-payment by the borrowers	The US Development Credit Authority provides loan portfolio guarantees for energy efficiency projects in Georgia (50% ceiling and eight-year guarantee). EIB and European Investment Fund (EIF), through its InnovFin products, also provide SMEs with a guarantee of up to 50% of a portfolio of new or existing loans.
Public investment	Grant	Concessional funds allocation	Development finance institutions and bilateral donor institutions often provide grants for interest or technical assistance for (e.g. green credit line products). The government (e.g. Enterprise Georgia) provides financial assistance to interest loans and collateral requirement to SMEs.
	Blending	Strategic use of public (generally concessional) and for-profit funding to catalyse private sector investment	For Shuakhevi hydropower project, IFC together with private-sector companies (Tata Power and Norway's Clean Energy Group) are equity sponsors, while EBRD and ADB provide senior loans. MIGA provides investment guarantee. Georgian government bears financial liabilities associated with the PPA.
	Cornerstone stake	Investment in an offering that occurs early in the investment process to increase chances of success and to play a demonstration role to attract other investors	The Global Energy Efficiency and Renewable Energy Fund (GEEREF) takes cornerstone stake in the Caucasus Clean Energy Fund to catalyse private-sector finance in small to medium hydropower projects.
	Fund seeding	Public investment to help establish private equity funds that specialise in green projects.	Georgian government established a state-owned JSC Georgian Energy Development Fund (GEDF) to provide equity investment in renewable energy projects. GEDF is in principle meant to have only a minority stake in a project.

ADB: Asian Development Bank; **EBRD**: European Bank for Reconstruction and Development; **EIB**: European Investment Bank; **MIGA**: Multilateral Investment Guarantee Agency.

Note: The range of risk mitigation instruments (or risk mitigants) and transaction enablers (e.g. securitisation and warehousing) that can help mobilise green finance is broader than those listed above. For more information, see e.g. OECD (2015), *Mapping Channels to Mobilise Institutional Investment in Sustainable Energy.*

Source: Author's analysis, based on GNIA (2015), GEEREF (2016), Adler (2017), EIF (2017), EU4Business (2017) and GEDF (2017).

The Green for Growth Fund (GGF) supports JSC TBC Bank by creating a subordinated fund for energy efficiency and renewable energy. The GGF leverages donor funding to mobilise finance from development banks and, ultimately, the private sector. An example of possible subordination is shown as follows (EU4Business, 2017):

- First loss tranche is provided by donors and different governments.
- Mezzanine tranche is provided by development banks.

- Senior tranche is provided by development banks and/or private institutional investors.
- (Technical assistance covers capacity building, awareness raising and market enabling activities, and validation and monitoring of energy savings and GHG emission reductions).

The US Development Credit Authority and the Multilateral Investment Guarantee Agency (MIGA of the World Bank Group) support investment in projects in Georgia. They have a range of guarantee instruments, such as partial credit guarantees, loan portfolio with credit guarantees, political risk insurance and investment guarantees for equity sponsors. The country has no export credit agency to date. However, JSC Partnership Fund and SACE (Cassa Depositi e Prestiti Group – the Italian export credit agency) are working together to establish a Georgian Export Credit Agency. As of September 2017, the partners were in the last stage of government approval (Partnership Fund, 2016).

The government also provides public investment through targeted grants or equity investment. A fully state-owned equity fund, the Georgian Energy Development Fund (GEDF), supports clean energy project development (e.g. wind, solar and hydropower). It either invests directly in early project development or offers government shares in GEDF to potential investors (GEDF, 2017). While not limited to green investment, Enterprise Georgia provides a 10% co-financing of bank loan interest rates and 12% for the annual interest rate of leasing for 24 months. It also provides a partial collateral guarantee of up to 50% for the first 48 months, among other services (Enterprise Georgia, 2017). Such support is provided only to loans in Georgian Lari in light of the government's effort to mitigate dollarisation of assets in the country (Enterprise Georgia, 2017).

Risk mitigation instruments will play an even greater role in expediting green finance mobilisation for the next decade to meet targets on Georgia's climate and green growth agendas. This is especially true for the short- and medium-terms (2020-30). A comprehensive stocktaking and review of risk mitigation instruments available in the country will be useful. It would help Georgia make the best use of available instruments and identify important risks not adequately covered (OECD, 2016a).

Based on the stocktaking, the government could select risk mitigation instruments against an agreed set of climate and non-climate criteria. This could help the country minimise the risk of arbitration and economic inefficiency (CPLC, 2017). Examples of such criteria (e.g. IPCC, 2014; CPLC, 2017) could include:

- immediate benefits of avoided GHG emissions, and other environmental aspects such as air pollution prevention, agriculture productivity increase, greater energy security and lower vulnerability to fossil fuel prices
- acceleration of technological change and positive spill-overs on innovations
- short-term knock-on effects and long-term development benefit (redirecting financial flows towards productive investments; strengthening industrial productivity; better access to energy, transport, and housing infrastructure; reducing poverty).

Considering development of a Georgian green bank or fund

There is neither a formally established national development bank nor a green investment bank[1] in Georgia. That said, the government and sovereign funds such as the Georgian Energy Development Fund and the Partnership Fund have certain functions of a development bank in financing projects with higher risks. However, these funds lack the scale and scope to make massive changes to financial flows towards climate and green growth agendas, especially in underserved sectors or companies (e.g. SMEs).

NEEAP proposes establishing an agency that delivers grants to mobilise public and private sector investment in energy efficiency, as well as donor co-ordination, amongst others (NEEAP Expert Team, 2017). LEDS proposes establishment of a Georgian Green Investment Bank either as part of the Partnership Fund or the Georgian Energy Development Fund, or a newly created one (Winrock and Remmisia, 2017). The Georgian Municipal Development Fund or Enterprise Georgia are not financial institutions or mandated to support green investment. However, their mandate could be extended to deliver risk mitigation instruments to climate- and environment-related investments.

In either case, a review of existing public financing mechanisms in Georgia would be a useful first step. A comprehensive approach to deploy risk mitigation instruments could catalyse private-sector investments in climate action. Such an approach should not fragment financial mechanisms and crowd out private-sector finance; see also OECD (2016a). Such a review could also assess whether some Georgian national funding entities can aggregate large numbers of smaller projects to reduce risk and gain access to international capital markets (Studart and Gallagher, 2016). Still, national development banks in general also face challenges about the effectiveness of their interventions. These challenges include the risk of market distortions arising from picking winners or from crowding-out effects; the potentially high opportunity costs associated with subsidised loans; and inefficiency due to the low level of scalability of projects (Torres and Zeidan, 2016; OECD, 2017a).

A clear political signal, mandate and guidance would help some public entities more legitimately explore and scale up investment in climate action. These entities include the Municipal Development Fund, Enterprise Georgia and the Partnership Fund. Capacity building would also be required for a wide range of issues. These include defining the scope of interventions (what kind of projects/entities to support); developing project appraisal criteria; and setting up methodologies to monitor projects and conditions attached to them, as well as to evaluate results. Better reporting and disclosure of information on interventions and their outcomes would also be useful to scale up and replicate successful interventions, and address similar challenges (Kato et al., 2014).

Competition policies

Developing an open and competitive electricity market

Open, competitive and unbundled electricity markets, if designed properly, create more space for renewable energy in developing countries (OECD, 2015). Georgia has a well-functioning power sector in general, but multiple organisations have concluded that creating a more competitive and transparent electricity market remains a critical challenge to the country (ADB, 2015; Kochladz et al., 2015; Energy Community Secretariat, 2017). Becoming a Contracting Party to the Treaty establishing the Energy Community (Energy Community Treaty) in July 2017 and the legislative frameworks of the EU Association Agreement are already driving the competitive and transparent electricity market in the country. This is leading Georgia to amend legislation in the energy sector to comply with the relevant EU Directives and further attract investment in the energy market.

Specifically, over-regulation of energy prices (e.g. on Enguri and Vardinili power plants) and insufficient competition have hindered development of transparent and competitive energy markets in Georgia (ADB, 2015; Pavlenishivili and Biermann, 2016; Energy Community Secretariat, 2017). EU Directives, particularly Directive 2009/72/EC on

Internal Market in Electricity, dictate abandoning tariff regulation and promoting market-based prices (Energy Community Secretariat, 2017). Georgia is not compliant with these directives. While the country has made progress, information on a range of supply costs of, or actual charges for, electricity and related services is not necessarily available.

Georgia's electricity distribution and supply activities are not fully unbundled. Activities in the electricity sector are subject to licensing by the Georgian National Energy and Water Supply Regulatory Commission (GNERC – the national regulatory body). They are categorised into electricity generation, dispatch, transmission and distribution licences (Table 5.4). The long-term memoranda directly negotiated between the government and the relevant energy sector entities contradict EU principles outlined in the Electricity Directive and the Gas Directive of the Third Energy Package (European Commission, 2013; Kochladz et al., 2015). The electricity distribution companies supply electricity to customers. Rules do not allow customers to switch suppliers, except when purchasing electricity directly from small-scale power plants (up to 13 MW). Non-regulated, direct agreements between retail customers and small power plants are not common as of 2017 due largely to the absence of competition in the market.

Table 5.4. **The structure of Georgia's electricity market**

Elements of the energy sector	Actors and roles
Electricity generators	The government owns the two largest hydropower plants (Enguri and Vardnili) and Gardabani Thermal Power Plants, Qartli Wind Power Plant, which produce about one-third of total electricity supply. Other generators are privatised.
Transmitters	Transmitters control and maintain the electricity transmission network. JSC Georgian State Electrosystem (GSE) (100% state-owned), JSC Unified Energy System Sakrusenergo (50% state-owned) and Energotrans LLC (100% owned by GSE) are the licensees.
Distributors	Distributors distribute electricity to consumers countrywide. JSC Telasi and JSC Energo-Pro Georgia* are the distributors in Georgia. (*JSC Energo-Pro Georgia has become the owner of JSC Kakheti Energy Distribution since September 2017).
Direct customers	Direct customers are those whom generation licensees can sell electricity directly to. As of 2017, all customers that consume at least 1 KWh per year are eligible to register as direct customer, although there are not many direct customers to date.
Dispatcher	JSC Georgian State Electrosystem (GSE) is the only licensed dispatcher, and in charge of technical administration of the entire electricity system and provision for its reliability.
Electricity System Commercial Operator (ESCO)	ESCO is a state-owned company and its functions include trading with balance electricity and guaranteed capacity, setting up and operating unified database, etc.
Georgian National Energy and Water Supply Regulatory Commission (GNERC)	The national regulatory body is responsible for licensing activities related to electricity generation, dispatch, transmission and distribution.

Source: Adopted from BAG (2016), GNERC (n.d.) and Energy Community Secretariat (2017).

State-owned enterprises in the energy sector, such as the Electricity System Commercial Operator (ESCO), the Georgian State Electrosystem (GSE) and the Energotrans LLC can also promote the government's green growth agenda. Preferential financing and influencing policy via the board (Prag and Röttgers, 2017), could help push the agenda forward. However, such strategies should not be used to justify an uncompetitive energy market.

> **Box 5.1. The Energy Community**
>
> The Energy Community, established in 2007, brings together the European Union (EU) and its partnership countries, including Georgia, to create an integrated pan-European energy market. The integration is based on the Energy Community Treaty.
>
> By signing the Energy Community Treaty, the contracting Parties committed to implementing key EU energy laws and develop an adequate regulatory framework. They must also liberalise their energy markets in line with the Treaty acquis within a fixed timeframe. The markets cover gas, electricity and security of supply, as well as renewable, oil, energy efficiency, environment, competition and statistics.
>
> The Minister of Energy of Georgia signed the Protocol of the Accession of Georgia to the Energy Community Treaty in 2016, and Georgia became a full-fledged, Contracting Party in July 2017. In general, the Energy Community Treaty seeks to create a stable regulatory and market framework that will do the following:
>
> - Establish a stable regulatory and market framework that can attract investment in power generation and networks.
> - Create an integrated energy market allowing for cross-border energy trade and integration with the EU market.
> - Enhance the security of supply to ensure stable and continuous energy supply that is essential for economic development and social stability.
> - Improve the environmental situation in relation with energy supply in the region and foster the use of renewable energy and energy efficiency.
> - Develop competition at regional level and exploit economies of scale.
>
> *Source:* Energy Community Secretariat (n.d.), Energy Community Facts in Brief.

Access to the electricity grid

The Network Code stipulates the rules, procedures, relevant timeline and price for connection to transmission networks in Georgia (GNERC, 2014). It allows transmission licensees to refuse an application from generators for connection to the grid under two conditions. First, they can refuse if the nearest sub-station or transmission line lacks available capacity. Second, they can refuse if the connection would threaten the security or stability of the grid system. No critical barrier to the connectivity has been identified. However, the Energy Community Secretariat regularly reviews the status for compliance with relevant EU Directives.

Georgia's Electricity Market Rules grant renewable energy sources priority access to new cross-border interconnection lines. However, such priority does not apply in a uniform manner. Only electricity generated by power plants commissioned after 2010 can benefit from priority access (Energy Community Secretariat, 2017).

The Ten-Year Network Development Plan of Georgia for 2017-27 of GSE mentions a potential ceiling on the connected capacity of wind power of 100 MW by 2020. This ceiling would come into force if the grid is not upgraded and integrated into the European energy market (Energy Community Secretariat, 2017). However, total wind resource potential in Georgia is estimated at 1 500 MW and the Georgian Energy Development Fund's pipeline alone would already exceed 100 MW.

In 2016, the regulatory regime for net-metering was enacted. This allows retail customers to connect renewable energy sources with capacity of up to 100 kWh to the distribution network. In return, they receive compensation for electricity delivered to the grid. During the first year of introducing the mechanism, eight customers engaged in the net-metering scheme. The total installed capacity was 153 kWh (Energy Community Secretariat, 2017).

Addressing information gap and enhancing capacity

Georgia's first Biennial Update Report (submitted to UNFCCC) describes the lack of data on climate change-related information as chaotic, dispersed, inaccurate, outdated and unreliable. It is thus one of the biggest obstacles to climate change action in Georgia (GoG, 2016). This lack of data affects a range of sectors to be engaged in Georgia's green growth agenda. For example, in energy, data are lacking on potential energy saving performance. In transport, more knowledge is needed about cleaner vehicle fleets and public transportation systems. In agriculture, GHG emissions projection from the sector is unknown. Finally, in waste, information on amounts, types, disposal and use of wastes, is not clear (GoG, 2016).

As in many countries, lack of awareness and knowledge in Georgia is one of the biggest challenges to scaling up finance for climate action. Both providers of finance and their clients are often unaware of environmental impacts on their activities and their exposure to climate risks. Further, they are not familiar with technical options for reducing the risks. The credit line product under the EBRD-supported Energocredit for energy efficiency and renewable energy, for example, generated an important lesson. It revealed that better understanding among potential borrowers about energy-efficiency technologies and their cost-benefit profiles could have further expedited disbursement of the credits. Low level of awareness about available financial instruments and sources (in this case, the credit lines extended by EBRD) was also an issue.

Some local financial institutions have claimed that even for large-scale hydropower – a well-established technology in Georgia – lack of technical and engineering information often prevents smooth development of projects. For instance, insufficient hydro-meteorological information between 1998 and 2010 created technical risks for Georgian commercial banks and other investors and lenders for design and development of hydropower projects. Technical assessments for solar, wind, biomass and geothermal potentials across the country have either not yet begun or are ongoing. These include feasibility studies on solar energy potential by JSC Caucasus Solar Company. In addition, the EBRD is also conducting an assessment of a national-level potential for solar energy under its Georgian Low Carbon Framework as of August 2017.[2] See also Ministry of Energy (2017).

Enhancing data on the performance of completed climate-related projects across different asset classes would help both investors and their clients. With better data, they could make investment strategies and financial decisions, as well as scale up and replicate successful projects. A number of climate- and environment-related projects have been conducted in Georgia. For instance, there have been about 150 projects in Georgia, to which bilateral and multilateral providers of climate-related development finance committed their support over the period 2013-15 (OECD, 2017d). However, information on their effectiveness assessed through monitoring and evaluation processes is often not readily available. Such information includes financial performances and associated technical, political and financial risks of specific types of projects and activities.

Financial institutions still lack sufficient human resources with enough expertise in technologies and engineering skills for energy efficiency and renewable energy projects. The capacity gap is narrowing with support of development co-operation partners. However, the gap affects even large banks such as Bank of Georgia and TBC Bank. They still need human resources to identify and appraise green projects, and to manage financial operations.

Clients of financial institutions (e.g. end-borrowers) also often lack capacities. Key gaps include how to identify or choose best-suited technologies and equipment; develop business proposals; and report to financial institutions on environmental performance. Apart from poor knowledge of finance for climate action, Georgian households, companies and particularly SMEs have low financial literacy. This increases their credit risk in the eyes of commercial banks. For instance, lack of accurate financial statements and sound business plans make SME performance less transparent. This becomes a barrier for SMEs to access financial sources (OECD, 2016b).

The government could establish, or help establish, a central data depository. This could collect, collate and maintain information on loan-level data, performance track records, definitions of climate-related projects, technologies and hydro-meteorological data. Several countries are also active in setting up learning networks and platforms. These aim to improve information flows, raise awareness of benefits from green investment and good national and international practices, and enhance analytical capabilities. For instance, the People's Republic of China (hereafter "China") established the International Institute of Green Finance, which promotes green investment in Georgia through a range of analytical projects (CUFE, 2016). Sustainable Stock Exchanges Initiative (SSE) is a peer-to-peer learning platform among stock exchanges that collaborates with investors, regulators and companies. Together, they enhance corporate transparency and performance on environmental, social and corporate governance (ESG) issues and encourage sustainable investment. SSE has helped 33 exchanges develop their own guidance on ESG reporting as of the end of 2016 (SSE, 2016). The US Department of Energy and its National Renewable Energy Laboratory also support a solar securitisation initiative (Solar Access to Public Capital) that is now being extended to China (the Chinese PV Alliance) and Europe (RESFARM) (OECD, 2017b).

Notes

1. Possible rationales, mandates and financing activities of "green investment banks" are analysed, among others, in OECD (2016a), *Green Investment Banks: Scaling up Private Investment in Low-carbon, Climate-resilient Infrastructure*, OECD Publishing, Paris.

2. Further information can be found at www.ebrd.com/work-with-us/projects/psd/georgian-low-carbon-framework.html.

References

ADB (2015), *Assessment of Power Sector Reforms in Asia: Experience of Georgia, Sri Lanka and Vietnam: Synthesis Report*, Asian Development Bank, Mandaluyong City, Philippines, https://www.adb.org/documents/assessment-power-sector-reforms-asia-synthesis.

Adler, B. (2017), *Development Credit Authority Putting Local Wealth to Work in Asia*, presentation at Asia Clean Energy Forum, Manila, 8 June 2017, https://d2oc0ihd6a5bt.cloudfront.net/wp-content/uploads/sites/837/2017/06/04-Beth-Adler_Asia-DCA-Pitch-Deck.pdf (accessed 30 October 2017).

BAG (2016), *Electricity Sector: Overview*, Business Association of Georgia, Tbilisi, http://bag.ge/file.helix?i=427e322d-a7ea-48fc-a283-d27ee04ac0a2&r=P (accessed 30 October 2017).

Capital Markets Working Group (2015), *The Georgian Capital Market Diagnostic Study and Recommendations*, Capital Markets Working Group, Tbilisi, www.economy.ge/uploads/meniu_publikaciebi/ouer/CMWG_Diagnostic_Report_12_May_2015.pdf.

Chernyavskay, T. and M. van Waveren Horgervorst (2017), "Financing RECP measures at SMEs: An overlooked opportunity", presentation at International Conference: Unlocking Private Finance for Energy Efficiency and Greener, Low-Carbon Growth in the Eastern Partnership and Central Asia Countries, Brussels, 30 August 2017, https://www.slideshare.net/OECD_ENV/session-4-presentation-by-tatiana-chernyavskaya-and-marko-van-waveren-unido (accessed 30 October 2017).

CPLC (2017), *Report of the High-Level Commission on Carbon Prices – Carbon Pricing Leadership*, Carbon Pricing Leadership Coalition (CPLC), Washington, DC, https://www.carbonpricingleadership.org/report-of-the-highlevel-commission-on-carbon-prices/.

CUFE (2016), "The International Institute of Green Finance was launched at CUFE", *News Release*, 20 October 2016, Central University of Finance and Economics (CUFE), Beijing, http://en.cufe.edu.cn/news/94936.htm.

EIB (2016), *Georgia: Neighbourhood SME Financing*, European Investment Bank, Luxembourg, www.eib.org/attachments/efs/economic_report_neighbourhood_sme_financing_georgia_en.pdf.

EIF (2017), "EUR 50 million to benefit SMEs in Georgia as EIF and ProCredit Bank Georgia sign first InnovFin transaction", *News Release*, 2 March 2017, European Investment Fund, Luxembourg, www.eif.org/what_we_do/guarantees/news/2017/innovfin_procredit_georgia.htm (accessed 30 October 2017).

Energy Community Secretariat (2017), *Energy Governance in Georgia, Report on Compliance with the Energy Community Acquis*, www.euneighbours.eu/sites/default/files/publications/2017-08/ECS_Georgia_Report_082017.pdf.

Energy Community Secretariat (n.d.), "Energy Community Facts in Brief", webpage, https://www.energy-community.org/dam/jcr:737d594d-e541-4c0e-975b-b7fc937cfad1/EnC_factsheet.pdf (accessed 31 August 2017).

Enterprise Georgia (2017), *Access to Finance*, http://enterprisegeorgia.gov.ge/en/whatwedo/Access-to-finance?v=75 (accessed 30 October 2017).

EU4Business (2017), *Investing in SMEs in the Eastern Partnership Countries: Georgia Country Report*, EU4Business, Tbilisi, http://eu4business.com/files/medias/country_report_georgia.pdf.

European Commission (2013), "Ownership unbundling: The Commission's practice at assessing the presence of conflicts of interests including in financial advisors", *Staff Working Document*, No. SWD 2013/177, https://ec.europa.eu/energy/sites/ener/files/documents/swd_2013_0177_en.pdf.

Galt & Taggart (2017), *Regional Fixed Income Market Watch, 04 May 2017 version*, Galt & Taggart, Tbilisi, http://galtandtaggart.com/research/research-reports/.

GEDF (18 January 2017), "Georgian Energy Development Fund announces selection of investor for development of Zestaponi WPP project", Georgian Energy Development Fund Investors blog, http://gedf.com.ge/en/georgian-energy-development-fund-announces-selection-of-investor-for-devepolment-of-zestaponi-wpp-project/ (accessed 30 October 2017).

GEEREF (2016), *GEEREF Impact Report 2015: Catalysing EUR10 Billion of Clean Power*, Global Energy Efficiency and Renewable Energy Fund, Luxembourg, http://geeref.com/assets/documents/GEEREF%20IMPACT%20REPORT%202015_FINAL%20final_public.pdf.

GNERC (n.d.), "Organization History", webpage, Georgian National Energy and Water Supply Regulatory Commission, http://gnerc.org/en/about/istoria/org (accessed 28 September 2017).

GNERC (2014), *Report on Activities of 2014*, Georgian National Energy and Water Supply Regulatory Commission, Tbilisi, http://gnerc.org/files/wliuri%20angariSi/Anual_Report_Eng_opt.pdf.

GNIA (2015), "Tata Power: Adjaristsqali Georgia", webpage, Georgian National Investment Agency, Tbilisi, https://www.investingeorgia.org/en/keysectors/success-stories/tata-power-adjaristsqali-georgia.page (accessed 13 October 2017).

GoG (2016), *First Biennial Update Report on Climate Change*, Government of Georgia, Tbilisi http://unfccc.int/files/national_reports/non-annex_i_parties/ica/application/pdf/first_bur_-_georgia.pdf.

IPCC (2014), *Synthesis Report: Contribution of Working Groups I, II and III to the Fifth Assessment Report of the Intergovernmental Panel on Climate Change*, Intergovernmental Panel on Climate Change, Geneva, www.ipcc.ch/report/ar5/syr/.

JSC National Bank of Georgia (2017), "Prospectus: Joint Stock Company Bank of Georgia: GEL 500,000,000 11.00% Notes due 2020", 30 May 2017, https://www.centralbank.ie/docs/default-source/Regulation/prospectus-regulation/2017/prospectusdocs-2017-05/314768-prospectus---standalone-pdf3057c7134644629bacc1ff0000269695.pdf?sfvrsn=0.pdf?sfvrsn=0.

Kato, T. et al. (2014), "Scaling up and replicating effective climate finance interventions", in *OECD/IEA Climate Change Expert Group Papers*, Vol. 2014/1, OECD Publishing, Paris, http://dx.doi.org/10.1787/5jslqffvmnhk-en.

Khaindrava, N. (2017), "Georgian Energy Development Fund", presentation at workshop on green finance mobilisation, Tbilisi, 22 June 2017, https://www.slideshare.net/OECD_ENV/session-3-presentation-by-georgian-development-fund (accessed 13 October 2017).

Kochladz, M. et al. (2015), *Georgia and European Energy Community – The Challenges of EU Integration*, Green Alternative, Tbilisi, https://greenalt.org/wp-content/uploads/2015/06/Georgia_and_European_Energy_Community.pdf.

Martikian, L. (24 April 2017), "EBRD initiates first-ever Eurobond issued in Georgian local currency", European Bank for Reconstruction and Development News blog, www.ebrd.com/news/2017/ebrd-initiates-firstever-eurobond-issued-in-georgian-local-currency.html.

Ministry of Energy (2017), *More Renewables and Improved Energy Efficiency: Energy Policy in Georgia*, Ministry of Energy of Georgia, Tbilisi, https://www.unece.org/fileadmin/DAM/env/documents/2017/WAT/04Apr_11_5SC/GE_5SC_Arabidze_EN.pdf.

MoESD (2016), *Capital Market Development Strategy*, Ministry of Economy and Sustainable Development with the Ministry of Finance and the National Bank of Georgia, Tbilisi.

National Bank of Georgia (2017a), *Statistical Data*, National Bank of Georgia, Tbilisi, www.nbg.gov.ge/index.php?m=304#monetarystatistics.

National Bank of Georgia (2017b), *Key Macroeconomic Indicators and International Ratings 2011-16*, National Bank of Georgia, Tbilisi, https://www.nbg.gov.ge/index.php?m=494.

National Bank of Georgia (2016), "Frequently Asked Questions Regarding the Program on Larization of Loans", webpage, https://www.nbg.gov.ge/index.php?m=339&n=&newsid=2985 (acccessed 9 August 2017).

NEEAP Expert Team (2017), *Draft National Energy Efficiency Action Plan*, report commissioned by European Bank for Reconstruction and Development, London.

OECD (2017a), *Investing in Climate, Investing in Growth*, OECD Publishing, Paris, http://dx.doi.org/10.1787/9789264273528-en.

OECD (2017b), *Mobilising Bond Markets for a Low-Carbon Transition*, OECD Publishing, Paris, http://dx.doi.org/10.1787/9789264272323-en.

OECD (2017c), *Workshop on Green Finance Mobilisation in Georgia – OECD*, www.oecd.org/environment/outreach/greenfinancemobilisationingeorgia.htm.

OECD (2017d), *Climate-related development finance data at the activity level reported to the OECD DAC Creditors Reporting System (CRS)*, www.oecd.org/dac/stats/climate-change.htm (acessed 30 October 2017).

OECD (2016a), *Green Investment Banks: Scaling up Private Investment in Low-carbon, Climate-resilient Infrastructure*, OECD Publishing, Paris, http://dx.doi.org/10.1787/9789264245129-en.

OECD (2016b), *Recommendations for Georgia's SME Development Strategy 2016-2020 March 2016 Project Report Working Group on SME Development Strategy*, OECD Publishing, Paris.

OECD (2015), *Policy Guidance for Investment in Clean Energy Infrastructure: Expanding Access to Clean Energy for Green Growth and Development*, OECD Publishing, Paris, http://dx.doi.org/10.1787/9789264212664-en.

Partnership Fund (14 June 2016), "Partnership Fund launches Ytong energy efficient block factory project", JSC Partnership Fund News and Media blog, www.fund.ge/eng/view_news/736 (accessed 30 October 2017).

Pavlenishivili, L. and F. Biermann (10 May 2016), "No price caps in the electricity wholesale market!", The Financial Opinion and Blogs, https://www.finchannel.com/opinion/57148-no-price-caps-in-the-electricity-wholesale-market (accessed 30 October 2017).

Prag, A. and D. Röttgers (2017), *State-Owned Enterprises and the Low-Carbon Transition*, OECD Publishing, Paris.

SSE (2016), *2016 Results and Impact Report: Sustainable Stock Exchanges Initiative*, Sustainable Stock Exchanges Initiative, www.sseinitiative.org/wp-content/uploads/2012/03/2016-Impact-Report_v4.pdf.

Studart, R. and K. Gallagher (2016), "Infrastructure for sustainable development: The role of national development banks", *Policy Brief*, No. 007 10-2016, Boston University, Global Economic Governance Initiative, www.bu.edu/pardeeschool/files/2016/08/Infrastructure.Sustainable.Final_.pdf.

Torres, E. and R. Zeidan (2016), "The life-cycle of national development banks: The experience of Brazil's BNDES", *The Quarterly Review of Economics and Finance*, Vol. 62, Elsevier, Amsterdam, pp. 97-104, http://dx.doi.org/10.1016/j.qref.2016.07.006.

Van Bilsen, J. (16 January 2017), "Green Bond Market in Georgia – a Growing Opportunity" Georgia Today on the Web News blog, http://georgiatoday.ge/news/5609/Green-Bond-Market-in-Georgia-%E2%80%93-a-Growing-Opportunity (accessed 30 October 2017).

Wing, I. and G. Timilsina (2016), *Technology Strategies for Low-Carbon Economic Growth: A General Equilibrium Assessment*, World Bank, Washington, DC, http://dx.doi.org/10.1596/1813-9450-7742.

Winrock and Remmisia (2017), "Georgia Low Emission Development Strategy Draft Report", commissioned by USAID-funded EC-LEDS Clean Energy Program, Winrock International and Sustainable Development Center, Remissia, Tbilisi.

ORGANISATION FOR ECONOMIC CO-OPERATION AND DEVELOPMENT

The OECD is a unique forum where governments work together to address the economic, social and environmental challenges of globalisation. The OECD is also at the forefront of efforts to understand and to help governments respond to new developments and concerns, such as corporate governance, the information economy and the challenges of an ageing population. The Organisation provides a setting where governments can compare policy experiences, seek answers to common problems, identify good practice and work to co-ordinate domestic and international policies.

The OECD member countries are: Australia, Austria, Belgium, Canada, Chile, the Czech Republic, Denmark, Estonia, Finland, France, Germany, Greece, Hungary, Iceland, Ireland, Israel, Italy, Japan, Korea, Latvia, Luxembourg, Mexico, the Netherlands, New Zealand, Norway, Poland, Portugal, the Slovak Republic, Slovenia, Spain, Sweden, Switzerland, Turkey, the United Kingdom and the United States. The European Union takes part in the work of the OECD.

OECD Publishing disseminates widely the results of the Organisation's statistics gathering and research on economic, social and environmental issues, as well as the conventions, guidelines and standards agreed by its members.

www.ingramcontent.com/pod-product-compliance
Lightning Source LLC
Chambersburg PA
CBHW082353220526
45470CB00008B/2731